# Dynamics

# Of

# Holiness

*Understanding your dominion over sin*

DYNAMICS OF HOLINESS

ISBN 978-2480-03-7

Published in Nigeria by:
**DOMINION PUBLISHING HOUSE**

**DOMINION PUBLISHING HOUSE**
38, Raji Oba Street, Iyana Ipaja, Alimosho
P.M.B. 21688, Ikeja, Lagos, Nigeria.
Tel: 01-4922067

All Scripture quotations are from the King James
Version of the Bible, except otherwise stated.

# CONTENTS

# Introduction

Righteousness exalteth a nation: but sin is a reproach to any people.

Proverbs 14:34

People of God, I want to get you on a hot frequency
that will keep you hot the remaining days of your life!

God is saying something to the Church.

As God began to speak about Double Honour for the
Church, I asked Him, "What is it that guarantees
consistent and never-ending honour?" He said:

**Tell them, honour is rooted in righteousness.**

And straightaway I began the teaching on holiness.

The following day, I got a copy of Kenneth Copeland's
30th anniversary publication of *The Believer's Voice of
Victory* (January 1997) from the mails. And what did
I see?

On the first page, Gloria Copeland was saying, *"Holiness is the pathway to God's glory"*. And she went on to say
that beginning from 20th of January, she would begin to
teach on the subject of holiness on their daily radio
broadcast, from Andrew Murray's book *The Holiest of All.*
That's a very unique coincidence!

Friends, heaven is sounding an alarm! God is
blowing a trumpet from heaven to the body of Christ!

5

There's a definite, very certain trumpet blowing from the throne of God!

God is crying out: *Holiness! Holiness! Holiness Unto God!*

There's a trumpet sounding now, preparing the Church for her hour of glory. That trumpet is saying:

*If you will be holy, I will make you whole — spirit, soul and body. I will cause you to excel, and make you shine as the brightness of the firmament, and as the stars of heaven forever and ever.*

Hear me friends, the Church is rising out of her "debris" and her filth, and taking her place in true holiness unto God. It's time!

Let me show you another prophetic link from as far back as 1961 (as contained in Charles and Frances Hunters' book, *How To Heal The Sick* (1983) pg. 8-16).

Last year, I mysteriously laid hold of a prophecy given by Tommy Hicks in 1961, describing a vivid vision of the body of Christ in the end–time:

> **Suddenly, I beheld what looked like a great giant, and as I stared and looked at it, I was almost bewildered by the sight. It was so gigantic and so great.**

He's talking about the gigantic status of the end–time Church. Remember Joel 2 talks about

...a great people and a strong; there hath not been

ever the like...a strong people set in battle array...And the Lord shall utter his voice before his army; for his camp is great...

That's where we belong!

Tommy Hicks continued:

*His feet seemed to reach to the north pole and his head to the south. It's arm were stretched from sea to sea. I could not even begin to understand whether this be a mountain or this be a giant, but as I watched, I suddenly beheld a great giant. I could see his head was struggling for life. He wanted to live...*

Do you really want to live? The soul that sinneth shall die! That's what God's Word says. So why are you playing with sin and claiming that you want to live?

According to this prophecy, this end–time Church will have a desire to rise, and that desire will generate the force to rise. And with that force, hell will loose its grip! And the Church will lift up her head one more time. Light will come, and with the coming of that light, the force needed for this great army to rise and to live, will be generated! And the beauty of the Church will emerge! (Isa. 60:1).

The prophesy continued:

*...but his body was covered with debris from head to foot, and at times this great giant would move his body and act as though it would even raise up at times. And*

7

*when it did, thousands of little creatures seemed to run away. Hideous creatures would run from this giant, and when he would become calm, they would come back. All of a sudden this great giant lifted his hand toward the heaven, and then it lifted its other hand, and when it did, these creatures by the thousands seemed to flee away from this giant and go into the darkness of the night.*

All hell loosed its grip of him. All hell will loose its grip of your life this hour!

*Slowly, this great giant began to rise and as he did, his head and hands went into the clouds. As he rose to his feet he seemed to have cleansed himself from the debris and filth that was upon him, and he began to raise his hands into the heavens as though praising the Lord, and as he raised his hands, they went even unto the clouds.*

When holiness takes a strong grip on every man and woman in the body of Christ, the rise of the Church will be so terrific!

*Suddenly, every cloud became silver, the most beautiful silver I have ever known.*

That's talking about the inexplicable, unbeatable beauty that God has packaged for the end–time Church, which purity will cause to manifest. What a day we have come into!

This prophecy given 36 years ago is talking about the Church to which you and I belong. That's the army of the Lord rising. You will not miss your place in it!

The Church will consciously, deliberately, determinedly and "choicefully" cleanse herself from every "debris" and filth, and lift up her head (like the prodigal son) and say, "No! I will arise and go! Home is sweeter than this pig sty!"

I'd like to announce to you that our Father's house is sweeter than the sweetest place on this earth! To miss that, with your eyes wide open, makes you the biggest fool of all ages!

Friends, the beauty of "Israel" is just being unfolded. And God is calling the body of Christ unto purity, so everybody can become a partaker of this sudden beauty, which has right now begun to come upon quite a number already.

God is saying something very strong to the Church today—it's time to clean up!

That prophecy said:

> *He wanted to livze, but his body was covered with debris from head to foot...*

That's a picture of the Church, the end–time army, the great army of God, presently pressed down with filthiness. Pressed down with immorality. Pressed down with lies, financial corruption, bribery, covetousness, idolatry, name it!

But at last this great giant rose!  You will rise!

If you want to see the beauty that God has in store for you in this end–time, it's time to go after purity.

> Follow peace with all men, and holiness, without which no man shall see the Lord.
>
> Hebrews 12:14

God is saying to His body on the earth now:

*Clean up!  I want to beautify you.*

Until you have cleaned up, you don't qualify for clean clothes, do you?  Until you go take "a bath", God won't put new clothes on you.  The glory that awaits the Church demands that we clean up first.

God is dangerously determined to beautify Zion, for the time for that marriage is set (Rev. 19:7-8).  Everyone that cleans up will be part of the bride. But everyone that says "It doesn't matter!" will be forgotten.

Everyone who will embrace the life of holiness will be a practical demonstrator of the beauty and glory of this end–time. Everyone that will say "No!" to the king's food (Dan. 1:8), everyone that will say "No!" to Potiphar's wife (Gen. 39:7-9), everyone that will say "No!" to Delilah (Jud. 16), everyone that will say "No!" to the Gehazi spirit (2 Kings 5), everyone that will say "No!" to the Ananias and Sapphira syndrome, (Acts 5), will be numbered among the shining stars of this end–time.

Friends, heaven is certain! But it takes holiness to get there. Likewise, this earth can be exciting for any child of God. But it takes holiness to have that excitement.

Hear this again: every move of God is preceded by a trumpet. And like 1 Corinthians 14:8 asks:

> For if the trumpet give an uncertain sound, who shall prepare himself to the battle?

Every battle is preceded by a trumpet. Right now, there is a trumpet sound blowing from heaven, to get the saints ready for the last onslaught against the kingdom of darkness; and we are privileged of God not to be left behind.

The SIN question is the barrier now between the body and its Chief Commander, the Lord Jesus Christ Himself.

When the SIN question is dealt with, this present strong wave of glory and power in the Church will cover the earth. Oh, yes, it will!

Every time a trumpet is sounding, it's to prepare you for what lies ahead. Watch out! We are in the last days, and one of the traps of the last days is the trap of unholiness.

2 Timothy 3:1 warns us:

> ...in the last days perilous times shall come.

I'd like you to open up! God is doing something

**11**

right now. God has been speaking about the new move all this while. Now the move has begun!

What we call revival is God's presence coming down in the midst of men (Zeph. 3:15). And God does not come until the way is prepared for His coming. May your life be prepared for His coming!

See this typical account in Exodus 19:

> And the Lord said unto Moses, Lo, I come unto thee in a thick cloud, that the people may hear when I speak with thee, and believe thee for ever. And Moses told the words of the people unto the Lord.
>
> And the Lord said unto Moses, Go unto the people, and sanctify them today and tomorrow, and let them wash their clothes.
>
> And be ready against the third day: for the third day the Lord will come down in the sight of all the people upon mount Sinai.
>
> And Moses went down from the mount unto the people, and sanctified the people; and they washed their clothes.
>
> And he said unto the people, Be ready against the third day: come not at your wives.
>
> Exodus 19:9-11,14-15

This shows the level of sanctification needed to welcome His majestic presence. He's here already. Just for you to open up, so that you can be a part of this glorious, mighty move, that's what we're talking about.

The children of Israel washed their clothes as they were instructed, and you know the rest of the story:

> And mount Sinai was altogether on a smoke, because the Lord descended upon it in fire: and the smoke thereof ascended as the smoke of a furnace, and the whole mount quaked greatly.
>
> Exodus 19:18

God's presence is the seal for His great acts amongst His people. And it takes the sanctification of a people for God's presence to come down without casualties. You will not be a casualty in these times we're in!

God said:

> Sanctify them today and tomorrow and the third day...Tell them, clean up! Clean up!! Clean up!!! He that will come is on the way!

And verse 14 says:

> ...and they washed their clothes

Friends, God's presence will distinguish His saints these end–times. The word "saint" will come back to the true Church. People would be called, Saint Joseph, Saint Paul, Saint Victor, etc. This will be by reason of our "stainless" walk with God.

Sanctify them today and tomorrow...

Holiness is double sanctification. It's knowing it and walking in it. These endtimes, the Church will march gallantly into the realms of "stainless" holiness.

Friends, let's wake up! Something is happening here! There's a strong trumpet from heaven saying:

> **I am going to come down. I am going to differentiate between my own, between the righteous and the wicked; between him that serveth God and him that serveth him not (Malachi 3:18).**

May you fall into the positive side!

We're in a healing season, for the establishment of glory in the body of Christ. It's time to brace up and take your place in this wild move. It's a possibility! God has shown us examples.

Sin is destructive; righteousness is constructive. Let's begin to demonstrate the nature of Christ by manifesting practical holiness in our thoughts, words and actions.

To be lawless is to be lifeless!

Holiness is a covenant treasure of the saints of God. I'm talking about blazing holiness! It is holiness for wholeness. Listen friends, God is visiting His body with the Spirit of holiness. Our sonship will be manifested in holiness. And the world is waiting!

Let's come to our sonship, and stop struggling at the level of servanthood. When the sons of God appear, the earth will tremble!

It is that sonship that God is building this hour, by the Spirit of holiness. Every act of God has a foundation. Psalm 11:3 says:

> If the foundations be destroyed, what can the righteous do?

What is the foundation for power? What is the foundation for the supernatural, (which is going to characterise the end–time Church)? It is very clear:

The foundation of God for man is RIGHTEOUSNESS!

We are talking about the release of power! We are talking about the manifestation of the sons of God! It's time to decide in which camp to be.

For everything there is a time (Eccl. 3:1). The Church is now in the hour of her sanctification, in preparation for her manifestation. If you miss this hour of sanctification, you are heading towards destruction unknowingly! It's time to live His life.

Before Jesus comes, the fear that people now have for the devil will be shifted to the Church. The Church of Jesus Christ will command the fear of all that dwell on the earth, by reason of the enormity of power manifestation, coming out of the realms of PURITY that the Church will be walking in.

We're training up to be part of that glorious army. All we need do is to awake to RIGHTEOUSNESS, and like good soldiers, endure whatever manner of hardness that will arise as a result. It's war time! That's what the trumpet is saying.

So, brace up! Get set! Or you'll be a casualty.

This message is not sent to anybody else, it's sent to YOU!! You in person! To get you set, lest you become a casualty, as the war intensifies. Whatever you must have heard before in this light, let's call it fun. It is now war! Therefore, watch out, sir!

Jesus looked over Jerusalem and wept, because they knew not the time of their visitation:

> And when he was come near, he beheld the city, and wept over it,
>
> Saying, If thou hadst known even thou, at least in this thy day, the things which belong unto thy peace! but now they are hid from thine eyes.
>
> For the days shall come upon thee, that thine enemies shall cast a trench about thee, and compass thee round, and keep thee in on every side,
>
> And shall lay thee even with the ground, and thy children within thee; and they shall not leave in thee one stone upon another; because thou knewest not the time of thy visitation.

Luke 19:41-44

If you miss the time of your visitation, you end up in destruction! Be sensitive! Something is about to break loose in your life!

God is visiting the earth now, to prepare the body of Christ for the last onslaught against the kingdom of darkness. It is our time!

When you're ignorant of your time of visitation you end up in devastation. Sir, what we have going on now is a divine visitation, to deliver from destruction! It is so clear! So real!

This trumpet sounding is for us. It is for our final preparation. You shall not be destroyed!

You need a turn around. That's why God has come around with this visitation mystery. This visitation is for you! Not for your neighbour, or your husband, or your wife, or your boss. Don't look at somebody else!

There is something about you that you need to stop, or it will stop you in this great move! There is something in your hand you need to drop now, or it will drop you tomorrow! There is something you must disappoint now, or you will be the one disappointed tomorrow. God is not mocked!

This is a very strange trumpet sounding from the throne of God! Clean up! Time is running out! Before you are abandoned, abandon SIN! Now! If you don't abandon it now, you will be abandoned by God tomorrow!

God is about to enthrone the Church. And He did

not enthrone Jesus until He fulfilled all righteousness. We were told in Psalm 45:6-7:

> Thy throne, O God, is for ever and ever: the sceptre of thy kingdom is a right sceptre.

> Thou lovest righteousness, and hatest wickedness: therefore God, thy God, hath anointed thee with the oil of gladness above thy fellows.

God is determined to glorify His Church. Whosoever does not let shall be let, until he be taken out of the way (2 Thess. 2:7-8). That will not be you!

In this book, you will discover the way of escape, in Jesus name!

God does not only show us the problem, He also offers the solution. And we are here, in this timely book, looking into those solutions.

Heaven is sounding an alarm, for the Church to come out of corruption, and enter into MANIFESTATIONS.

In this book, God is offering you the treatment required. I want you to see the urgency, and give it all your attention. I'd like you to be awake! This is your hour of deliverance. God wants to bring you into a realm of purity that will establish your covenant beauty upon the earth, and make you the envy of your generation!

God is now set to release glory to His body, and they have to be set for Him, otherwise they will be destroyed by it. You will be raised by it! You will be lifted by it, in Jesus precious name!

Hear this: HOLINESS is an adventure, a possible adventure. Many have gone in the way of holiness, and are walking on the highways of life. You can go that way too.

SIN is not a friend, it's a destroyer any day! But PURITY is the booster of power! The whole creation is waiting for the manifestation of the sons of God. It's time to retrace our steps back home.

In this book, the Holy Ghost, this hour, is offering you treatments that will never let you become calm enough to let the hideous creatures lay hold on you again (as in Tommy Hicks' prophecy).

Remember Joshua the high priest in Zechariah 3:1-5? Satan stood by him to resist him and forced a filthy garment on him. But God brought him out. That same God is here this hour. If you sincerely want to, you too will come out.

Get set for an ENCOUNTER with the HOLINESS of God! Let His coal of fire touch you and renew you; refire you and put you back on your feet!

Sin has been having a field day, we must stop it before it stops us!

I have seen devastations and I'm scared! God is warning us: *Be holy, for I am holy!*

Romans 6:23 tells us:

For the wages of sin is death, but the gift of God is eternal life through Jesus Christ our Lord.

We will be celebrating that gift of eternal life, as we subdue sin and begin to punish the devil, who is "the man of sin".

This book is announcing that there is a wave of holiness that is coming upon the body of Christ, to prepare her for the final onslaught against Satan's dominion; which will cause us to take our place in destiny and bring God's people to their inheritance. Thank God we are not left behind!

I want you to open up right now and believe God this day for a hot desire for holiness.

Many are stranded, many are strangulated, life is becoming terribly unbearable for many — all because of sin! It's time to take your place in true holiness unto God.

Satan is out for us because we are precious. Let's stop him, now!

You will encounter the holiness of God in this book, and the fullness of His glory will be made manifest in your life henceforth, in Jesus precious name!

# 1

# Outstanding Prophetic Signals

And of the children of Issachar, which were men that had understanding of the times, to know what Israel ought to do; the heads of them were two hundred; and all their brethren were at their commandment.

1 Chronicles 12:32

Here we are face to face with the prophetic last days. An understanding of the times in which we live, will help our spiritual positioning, and enhance the much needed vigilance.

We are in the greatest days of the Church!

We are in the GOLDEN AGE OF ZION!

This army (the Church) God is raising in our days, there had never been its kind!

Joel 2:3-11 paints a very unique picture of this army:

A fire devoureth before them; and behind them a flame burneth; the land is as the garden of Eden before them, and behind them a desolate wilderness; yea, and nothing shall escape them.

The appearance of them is as the appearance of horses; and as horsemen, so shall they run.

Like the noise of chariots on the tops of mountains shall they leap, like the noise of a flame of fire that devoureth the stubble, as a strong people set in battle array.

Before their face the people shall be much pained: all faces shall gather blackness.

They shall run like mighty men: they shall climb the wall like men of war; and they shall march every one on his ways, and they shall not break their ranks.

Neither shall one thrust another; they shall walk every one in his path: and when they fall upon the sword, they shall not be wounded.

They shall run to and fro in the city; they shall run upon the wall, they shall climb up upon the houses; they shall enter in at the windows like a thief.

The earth shall quake before them; the heavens shall tremble: the sun and the moon shall be dark, and the stars shall withdraw their shining:

And the Lord shall utter his voice before his army:

for his camp is very great: for he is strong that executeth his word; for the day of the Lord is great and very terrible: and who can abide it?

What a glorious army!

What a people of affluence!

What an army of exploits!

What a people to be envied!

However, we also have other prophetic scriptures that call for extra vigilance on the part of this great army. The opposition from hell is great, but our victory is sure!

Listen friends, God showed me some outstanding prophetic pointers to the season we are into right now:

# A CHURCH OF UNIQUE STRENGTH

The Lord said unto my Lord, Sit thou at my right hand, until I make thine enemies thy footstool.

The Lord shall send the rod of thy strength out of Zion: rule thou in the midst of thine enemies.

Thy people shall be willing in the day of thy power, in the beauties of holiness from the womb of the morning: thou hast the dew of thy youth.

Psalm 110:1-3

From this we see that we are in the age of strength in the Church of our Lord Jesus Christ. And it really shows. We have diverse testimonies of the manifestation of power by seemingly ordinary men and women—going about armed with the manifold wisdom of God, healing the sick, raising the dead, delivering the insane, opening blind eyes —just devastating the kingdom of darkness!

We are in the day of His power!

Recently, a woman came to me in tears. She was heavy with pregnancy and was so disturbed. She had been told that the baby was coming out with the feet, so she would need to be operated on, to bring out the baby. I took her by the head and asked her to open her mouth. I breathed into her mouth and said, "You are going to deliver your baby now. Go!" And that was it!

On their way home from Church, labour started! They were forced to drive to the nearest clinic, and her husband rushed home to bring the things the baby would need. By the time he returned with the things, it was the cry of his baby that welcomed him!

We are in the day of His power! And what does that tell us?

The days of the manifestations of His power are also the days of temptation! Great temptations accompany mighty manifestations.

When Samson came on the scene in Israel with unusual strength, a great temptation of immorality came too, and destroyed his destiny! We are in the day of His power, we should be extra vigilant, to escape the traps of the devil.

Every manifestation of God attracts temptations from hell. So clean up! Time is running out!

The strength of the endtime Church, can be likened to a man called Samson in the Old Testament. As soon as that strength came on the scene, Satan said, "The only way to trap his strength is through immorality", and he succeeded.

Joel 2 also paints a picture of the endtime Church as a Church of a unique strength.

> ...a great people and a strong; there hath not been ever the like, neither shall be any more after it, even to the years of many generations.

> A fire devoureth before them; and behind them a flame burneth: the land is as the garden of Eden before them, and behind them a desolate wilderness; yea, and nothing shall escape them.

> The appearance of them is as the appearance of horses; and as horsemen, so shall they run.

> Like the noise of chariots on the tops of mountains shall they leap, like the noise of a flame of fire that devoureth the stubble, as a strong people set in battle array.

> Joel 2:2-5

**25**

That kind of strength was depicted in Samson. In Judges 15, we read an account of how he slew a thousand Philistines with the jawbone of an ass (verse 15-16). And in Judges 16:3, we also read:

> And Samson lay till midnight, and arose at midnight, and took the doors of the gate of the city, and the two posts, and went away with them, bar and all, and put them upon his shoulders, and carried them up to the top of an hill that is before Hebron.

But all that strength was devoured by the trap of immorality!

> And when Delilah saw that he had told her all his heart, she sent and called for the lords of the Philistines, saying, Come up this once, for he hath shewed me all his heart. Then the lords of the Philistines came up unto her, and brought money in their hand.
>
> And she made him sleep upon her knees; and she called for a man, and she caused him to shave off the seven locks of his head; and she began to afflict him and his strength went from him.
>
> And she said, The Philistines be upon thee, Samson. And he awoke out of his sleep, and said, I will go out as at other times before, and shake myself. And he wist not that the Lord was departed from him.
>
> Judges 16:18-20

We are in the days of the strength in Zion. The Lord is

sending the rod of His strength now, and the Delilahs are all over, the Jezebels are all over. We must be on our guard. We are in the days of the strength of God in Zion, we must see to it that the devil does not cast us down.

You have to be determinedly purposeful. Say to yourself, "I am going to walk this holy journey, it is a possible adventure. Others have gone on it and triumphed. I am going to go on it and attain".

Paul the apostle said:

> Ye are witnesses, and God also, how holily and justly and unblameably we behaved ourselves among you that believe.
>
> 1 Thessalonians 2:10

May this be your testimony also. You need a testimony of holiness, a testimony of victory over corruption and filthiness. When you get close to the Holy God, you will see how much you need to enhance your holiness in God.

Samson was a one–man army. Kingdoms feared his person. He could penetrate anywhere. He broke chains as though they were thread.

> ...and the Spirit of the Lord came mightily upon him, and the cords that were upon his arms became as flax that was burnt with fire, and his bands loosed from off his hands.
>
> Judges 15:14

27

He would uproot the gates and carry them along with the posts and climb the mountains! That time no razor had touched his head — his covenant with God was still intact.

If we would care to keep our covenant of purity with the Father, the least one among us will become like the house of David, and the house of David will operate in the class of God.

Purity is the booster of power!

> And every man that hath this hope in him purifieth himself, even as he is pure.
>
> 1 John 3:3

Look at this scripture in Proverbs 7:9-14:

> In the twilight, in the evening, in the black and dark night:
>
> And, behold, there met him a woman with the attire of an harlot, and subtil of heart.
>
> (She is loud and stubborn, her feet abide not in her house:
>
> Now is she without, now in the streets, and lieth in wait at every corner.)
>
> So she caught him, and kissed him, and with an impudent face said unto him,
>
> I have peace offerings with me; this day have I payed my vows.

Satan vowed through that woman to cast that man down. So the man also has to vow in God, to destroy the plan of Satan. It is your responsibility.

We are in a very great conflict, because the strength of the Church is now emerging, the scene is now set for the strength of Israel to manifest. That's why Satan has vowed to destroy the seed of Jesus. You must vow to destroy him! We must be very sensitive.

Samson, the strength of Israel, was slain on the laps of Delilah! The treasure of the earth became a toy for the heathen. A dagger pierced through his soul. As an ox goes to the slaughter and the bird to it's slayer, not knowing it was for life; so was the strength of Israel trapped by immorality, and his destiny, and the destiny of the nation that he represented, dashed on the rocks! *"How are the mighty fallen, and the weapons of war perished"* (2 Sam. 1:27).

If we are in our days of strength, then it should be our greatest moments of vigilance. 1 Peter 5:8 says:

Be sober, be vigilant; because your adversary the devil, as a roaring lion, walketh about, seeking whom he may devour.

Satan has no more news, he's the same old serpent. If he set traps of sexual immorality for Samson, you can be sure he has set it (heavily too) for this emerging great army.

So let's watch it!

# A CHURCH OF SUPER WISDOM

Unto me, who am less than the least of all saints, is this grace given, that I should preach among the Gentiles the unsearchable riches of Christ;

And to make all men see what is the fellowship of the mystery, which from the beginning of the world hath been hid in God, who created all things by Jesus Christ:

To the intent that now unto the principalities and powers in heavenly places might be known by the church the manifold wisdom of God.

Ephesians 3:8-10

We are also in the days of His wisdom. God is giving unique insights to His people here and there, for victories, triumphs and breakthroughs in every area of life.

There was a man called Solomon. He was the embodiment of manifold wisdom in the Old Testament. God said to him:

Wisdom and knowledge are granted unto thee; and I will give thee riches, and wealth, and honour, such as none of the kings have had that have been before thee, neither shall there any after thee have the like.

2 Chronicles 1:12

But this wisdom was converted to madness, through immorality.

1 Kings 3:3 testified concerning Solomon:

> And Solomon loved the Lord, walking in the statutes of David his father...

But see what 1 Kings 11:1-3 said:

> But king Solomon loved many strange women, together with the daughter of Pharaoh, women of the Moabites, Ammonites, Edomites, Zidonians, and Hittites;
>
> Of the nations concerning which the Lord said unto the children of Israel, Ye shall not go in to them, neither shall they come in unto you: for surely they will turn away your heart after their gods: Solomon clave unto these in love.
>
> And he had seven hundred wives, princesses, and three hundred concubines: and his wives turned away his heart.

And verse 4 says:

> For it came to pass, when Solomon was old, that his wives turned away his heart after other gods: and his heart was not perfect with the Lord his God, as was the heart of David his father.

They converted his wisdom to foolishness, and at the end of his journey, everything was vanity to him—

> The words of the Preacher, the son of David, king in Jerusalem.

> Vanity of vanities, saith the Preacher, vanity of vanities; all is vanity.
>
> Ecclesiastes 1:1-2

Solomon's many–sided wisdom was turned to foolishness on the laps of immorality!

Do you know the Church has never witnessed the level of wisdom she's witnessing now—that a church will stand out and build a university! Besides, there are lots of innovations, a lot of creativity going on in the body of Christ today, weights of amazing wisdom from heaven!

But Satan is used to the game. All these can be easily trapped and corrupted by immorality and converted to foolishness. He did it to Solomon.

Solomon loved the Lord, yes! But immorality turned his heart away, and God's anger replaced God's love. Verse 9 tells us:

> And the Lord was angry with Solomon, because his heart was turned from the Lord God of Israel, which had appeared unto him twice.

No one ever fought with God and prospered. No! The Lord was angry with Solomon, his peace was turned to unrest, his life was turned into shambles.

Friends, we are in the age of wisdom in the body of Christ, you must fight the trap of sin. You must wage war against the demon of immorality. You must fight it! If you don't fight it, it will floor you. If you don't fight it, it will destroy you! God forbid!

The wisdom of God in Solomon crashed on the altar of immorality, God's wisdom will not crash in your life.

We are in the age of the many–sided wisdom of God. Things are just happening! It is the age of practical wisdom. We have terrific proofs to show for it. For instance, there has not been an age where Christian homes are as peaceful as they are now. Why? The wisdom of God is reigning.

But inspite of this productive wisdom, the trap is still there. The demon of immorality is still at large much more than ever before. It must be destroyed! We are in the hour of wisdom, so the strange women are so many around. 1 Kings 11:1 said, "*But King Solomon loved many strange women*". And they turned his heart away from God. There's need for caution and godly fear. Immorality will take its toll among people this endtime.

Friends, immorality erodes intelligence, it mars wisdom. Don't be caught!

## THE WEALTHY CHURCH

And they shall be mine, saith the Lord of hosts, in that day when I make up my jewels; and I will spare them, as a man spareth his own son that serveth him.

*Malachi 3:17*

There's a day in God's book called the day of His jewels.

**33**

That is the day of prosperity for the Church of Jesus Christ. Also Haggai 2:9 makes us understand that:

> The glory of this latter house shall be greater than of the former, saith the Lord of hosts: and in this place will I give peace, saith the Lord of hosts.

So we are in the days of wealth in the Church. Before Jesus arrives back here, the Church will be in control of the economy of the whole world! There will be such levels of wealth in the body of Christ that the world has never known before.

Jesus said:

> For it is easier for a camel to go through a needle's eye, than for a rich man to enter into the kingdom of God.
>
> Luke 18:25

That tells you how you must brace up, if you must walk in that wealth and still make it through to heaven.

It takes some money to have 700 wives! It takes quite some possessions to be able to accommodate 700 wives! Solomon had all that. God gave it to him—

> ...and I will give thee riches, and wealth, and honour, such as none of the kings have had that have been before thee, neither shall there any after thee have the like.
>
> 2 Chronicles 1:12

But he was corrupted by it because he went messing with:

> ...strange women, together with the daughter of Pharaoh, women of the Moabites, Ammonites, Edomites, Zidonians, and Hittites:
>
> Of the nations concerning which the Lord said unto the children of Israel, Ye shall not go in to them, neither shall they come in unto you: for surely they will turn away your heart after their gods: Solomon clave unto these in love.
>
> 1 Kings 11:1-2

He built altars for all the gods of his wives!

Friends, it takes God for one to have money and not worship it.

Now that we are in the day of prosperity in the body of Christ, we must crave after purity, or plenty will become our regret.

The day of His jewels is for they that fear the Lord. Look at it in Malachi 3:16-18

> Then they that feared the Lord spake often one to another: and the Lord hearkened, and heard it, and a book of remembrance was written before him for them that feared the Lord, and that thought upon his name.
>
> And they shall be mine, saith the Lord of hosts, in that

day when I make up my jewels; and I will spare them, as a man spareth his own son that serveth him.

Then shall ye return, and discern between the righteous and the wicked, between him that serveth God and him that serveth him not.

Listen to me, we are in the most glorious times and the most perilous time as well. Oh yes! God is going to enrich His body, but if that riches lack purity, it will bring destruction and devastation! Solomon, the wealthiest, missed it eventually, not because of his wealth, but because his heart was turned away by the misuse of wealth.

That's why he said in his proverbs, "*cleave to the wife of your youth, don't afflict your destiny, like I've afflicted my own*" (Prov. 5:18 paraphrased).

Misuse of wealth will bring corruption. Solomon was the wealthiest, but he was the most corrupt! There is a day of wealth in the body of Christ. It is the latter day, under the latter rain—the time we're living in now. Prosperity is fast becoming our identity. Purity must become our crave, so that God will not be angry with us. The Bible says:

And the Lord was angry with Solomon...

1 Kings 11:9

The love of yesterday suddenly turned to anger! God will not be angry with you!

36

Immorality erodes dignity! It breaks a man's destiny. Watch it!

Comfort is the cheapest access to corruption. Wealth, when it is not operated by covenant, becomes corruption.

1 Timothy 6:9 says:

> But they that will be rich fall into temptation and a snare, and into many foolish and hurtful lusts, which drown men in destruction and perdition.

And verse 11 warns:

> But thou, O man of God, flee these things; and follow after righteousness, godliness, faith, love, patience, meekness.

We are in the days of wealth; but much more, there is a trap of sin laid for us. Satan has planted mines of immorality in the fields, waiting for people to run into them.

> Now the Spirit speaketh expressly, that in the latter times some shall depart from the faith, giving heed to seducing spirits, and doctrines of devils.
>
> 1 Timothy 4:1

So a lot of seducing spirits will be released as traps for the latter days saints of God. Satan will seduce you (operating with the doctrine of devils), to make you feel it's not dangerous, that it doesn't really matter, that it's nothing, after all everybody is doing it. That is the devil speaking!

Let us therefore test and examine ourselves and return to the Lord. Purity must become our target. Your "yea" must be "yea", and your "nay" must be "nay".

When plenty has become your identity, purity must be your target also, or that plenty will destroy you. The chances of the rich getting to heaven, Jesus said, is very slim, because they're so vulnerable to worldly corruptions, among which is immorality.

A man's life does not consist in the abundance of things that he possesses, but in the abundance of God, which he has.

Hear this again: now that plenty has become our identity, purity must become our desire; otherwise prosperity will become our destruction! God forbid!

Solomon, the most prosperous, eventually was the most vulnerable, and the greatest victim of sexual trap. Now that we are in the age of covenant wealth, we need covenant caution, so that we don't fall into destruction. God is opening these mysteries and seals to us, so we can stay on covenant guard against the traps of the wicked one.

# THE ANOINTING

Because of the savour of thy good ointments thy

name is as ointment poured forth, therefore do the
virgins love thee.

Song of Solomon 1:3

Also:

It shall come to pass afterwards, that I will pour
out my spirit upon all flesh...

Joel 2:28

So we are in the hour of unction for Zion, and the
virgins will be attracted to her.

When Jesus, the·most anointed came on the earth,
a lot of women were always around Him (Luke 8:2-3).
But none of them was on His staff. He had 12 solid
men that surrounded Him, to ward off both the devil
and human agents.

The anointing of the Holy Spirit naturally compels
attraction. And women are most given to such
attractions. Even when Jesus died, they were there!

The Bible promises us in Zechariah 10:1, that He will
give us both the former and the latter rain in the same
month. It is because of this anointing that is about to
come on you that God is now sounding an alarm, saying:
*"Be careful! Be cautious! There is death in the pot!"*

The more anointed you are, the more cautious you
should be.

Therefore do the virgins love thee.

We are now in the day of power.

You know strength and power are two different things. When strength is directed to accomplish a given task, it becomes power. It is reserved energy. But when it is now turned into activity, to produce certain ends, it becomes power. Power is the ability to do work. The ability is strength, the turning of the ability into action is called power.

We are now in the day of His power. Acts 1:8 says you shall receive power after the Holy Ghost has come upon you. Power! The power is so evident all around now. Power! *"Therefore do the virgins love thee"*. That's why they hang around you.

Never mind those women, they are not possessed as they claim. They are only being used by Satan, to set a trap for the anointed.

Do you know why God is sounding an alarm? Satan is out to use too many people to corrupt the lifting of the Church. You will not be caught!

## THE ESTABLISHED CHURCH

And it shall come to pass in the last days, that the mountain of the Lord's house shall be established in the top of the mountains, and shall be exalted above the hills; and all nations shall flow unto it.

And many people shall go and say, Come ye, and let us go up to the mountain of the Lord, to the house of the God of Jacob; and he will teach us of his ways, and we will walk in his paths: for out of Zion shall go forth the law, and the word of the Lord from Jerusalem.

Isaiah 2:2-3

The endtime Church will be exalted and established by God. So, as God establishes the Church, there is need for caution. Taste must be brought under control or regrets become the result.

God is establishing His kingdom in our time. That's why the churches are blossoming—the kingdom of God is growing. That's one reason why we have to be extra sensitive.

Look at David:

And David perceived that the Lord had established him king over Israel, and that he had exalted his kingdom for his people Israel's sake.

And David took him more concubines and wives out of Jerusalem, after he was come from Hebron: and there were yet sons and daughters born to David.

2 Samuel 5:12-13

Did you see the words *"established"* and *"exalted"*? When David entered that exalted realm, *he took him* more concubines and wives out of Jerusalem. His taste was corrupted by reason of establishment and exaltation. Promotion gave way to corruption, establishment twisted his taste.

**41**

We are now in the season of our establishment, in the seasons of our exaltation; it is therefore time to take caution. Liftings that could only come from heaven are now visiting the Church, it is time to take caution!

As soon as Satan saw that David's kingdom was established, he laid a trap of immorality against his destiny and trapped him! He *"took him more concubines and wives"!* So we have to be cautious.

All these prophetic pointers culminate in the fact that we need to clean up, because time is fast running out.

Clean up!  Time is running out!

We are the most privileged, yet the most vulnerable of all saints that ever lived.  We are living on the edge of creation.  And when you walk on the edge, you must be extra cautious, because any wrong step will pull you down to the bottomless pit!

We are children of prophets, and prophecies are being fulfilled in our time, we need caution therefore.

So, strength is not enough; wisdom is not enough; power is not enough; neither is wealth the answer; promotion and establishment is not the key either. It is caution. We need caution! We need to be sensitive! While God is excited, hell is envious, seeking opportunity and occasion against us.

We shall not be caught!

# 2

# Understanding The Move Of God

For if we live after the flesh, we shall die: but if ye through the Spirit do mortify the deeds of the body, ye shall live.

Romans 8:13

Every move of God is enhanced by the ministry of the Holy Spirit. He convicts both of sin and of judgement, and destroys the deeds of the flesh.

Sin is so subtle, but the Holy Spirit can cheaply arrest it.

Remember, God has not changed, His pattern remains the same. Now, come with me as we take an adventure into the move of God.

## REPENTANCE

The treatment for the sting of death is repentance.

He that covereth his sins shall not prosper: but

**43**

whoso confesseth and forsaketh them shall have mercy.

Proverbs 28:13

X Nothing works when sin is enthroned. I'd like you to be willing today to dethrone sin.

But as truly as I live, all the earth shall be filled with the glory of the Lord.

Because all those men which have seen my glory, and my miracles, which I did in Egypt and in the wilderness, and have tempted me now these ten times, and have not hearkened to my voice;

Surely they shall not see the land which I sware unto their fathers, neither shall any of them that provoked me see it.

Numbers 14:21-23

So God's mercy is limited. Continuity in sin can frustrate His grace. When temptation continues, it graduates into provocation, and when provocation is in place, condemnation is sure.

If you don't stop tempting Him, He will count it at a point as provocation. And when God is provoked, condemnation is inevitable.

If any man says he has no sin when he has sinned, he deceives himself. But when he confesses his sin, God is faithful and just, He will forgive him his sins and cleanse him from all unrighteousness (1 John 1:8-9).

So friends, to say it's not there when it's there, you are deceiving yourself. The end is destruction! The scriptures cannot be broken. God is no respecter of persons. Sin is sin, no matter who commits it.

> But God shall wound the head of his enemies, and the hairy scalp of such an one as goeth on still in his trespasses.
>
> Psalm 68:21

Continuity in sin is a destroyer of destiny.

Jesus told the devil:

> Thou shalt not tempt the Lord thy God.
>
> Matthew 4:7

So when we start tempting God, we have joined the devil in his ministry. Listen, that death has not struck yet does not mean it is not in view. Has God changed? He said, "*These ten times you have tempted me*". May that tenth time not meet you!

The reason God is saying this is because many are close to the tenth time now. So this might as well be the last chance they will ever have on earth. This might be the last opportunity they have!

Friends, no victim of sin has ever been known to escape! Repentance is the only way out. It is the highway to restoration. And restoration is the gateway to manifestation.

Repentance is the only way to recovery. Let's get back now, and put order back into our lives, and gather the shambles of our broken lives; so that at the gate you will not hear, "*I know ye not, ye that work iniquity*" (Matt. 7:23).

Nothing compares in beauty to heaven, where we are going to—our place of eternal abode. We can't afford to toy with it. Every unrepented sin is recorded in heaven's book.

In 2 Chronicles 15, beginning from verse 1, we see the restoration of Israel—how they made a covenant "*with all their heart and with the whole of their desire*", and God heard them, and their difficulties were levelled, their reproaches were removed. All their heart was there, all their desire was there, and God heard them!

For instance, the honour in marriage is "*the bed undefiled*" (Heb. 13:4). When the bed is defiled, prayer and fasting won't bring the honour, no matter how much you pray. It's only repentance that can bring restoration.

If you are in the house of sin as you're reading this, go right now, pack your things and leave that place!

If you're not married and you are living somewhere (with someone), go now and pack your luggage and sleep on the street if you must! It's better for you to be on the street and get to heaven, than to go to hell from a mansion!

Say like the prodigal son, "I will arise and go. My

redemption has come. I put on a new garment". If it is your choice, today will mark the end of that affliction and that plague in your life. Plead the blood of Jesus for your covering, for consecration, for purity, for holiness.

When sin stings and it's not treated, it results in death. For instance if you have a snake bite and you don't treat it, you are on your way to the grave. Repentance is God's covenant treatment for the sting of sin. Otherwise, it will result in death.

The Bible said he that committed sin is of the devil (1 John 3:8). And you know the devil is a serpent. He has a deadly venom inside him. When he bites and the bite is not treated, death is inevitable.

I see you rescued from the dungeons of death today!

Repent, before God strikes!

God is counting and waiting. He is not slow as some count slowness, but is longsuffering to us ward, not wishing that any should perish, but that all should come to repentance (2 Pet. 3:9).

When you continue in sin, your future is damned.

Stop now! Make a U-turn back to the holy God of wholeness. You are never made whole until you embrace holiness. Wholeness, (spirit, soul and body), is a result of a holy walk with God.

**Thou shalt not tempt the Lord your God.** When sin is unchecked, it is counted as tempting God. And when you tempt God, you have applied for His destruction! When they tempted Him in the wilderness, He destroyed them!

You will not be destroyed!

Sin is not a friend, it's an enemy! Therefore seek ye the Lord while He may be found. Call upon Him while He is still near.

The former things God has overlooked. But now He commands every man everywhere to repent. To repent!

Before sin finishes, finish it now. The kingdom of God suffereth violence, and the violent takes it by force (Matt. 11:12).

All hell is envious of you. Would you now slay your destiny to uncleanliness, unchastity, infidelity, sexual traps, financial impropriety? Would you crash your destiny to stealing? To lying? To bitterness and malice? God forbid!

Friends, the payday of sin is only averted by repentance—timely repentance.

Sin will never have God's approval. It was the reason He sent His only begotten Son to the world — to provide an everlasting solution to the curse of sin. We shall not frustrate His grace!

You can't afford to watch the devil tear you down. Sin has no dominion over you. Legally, sin has no hold on your destiny. Jesus paid the price. Paul said, "*ye are bought with a price*" (1 Cor. 7:23).

So legally, you belong to Jesus now, not to Satan "the man of sin". So Satan can't force you to sin, because you have been legally redeemed by the blood of the Lamb. You now belong to someone else.

When God makes known to you His words, He brings you to the realm of liberty "*Turn you at my reproof: behold, I will pour out my spirit unto you, I will make known my words unto you.*" (Prov. 1:23).

John 8:32 says, "*And ye shall know the truth, and the truth shall make you free*". That is, you will flow in revelations, when you turn at His reproof.

Jesus said: "*You are my friends, if you do whatever I tell you to do*" (John 15:14). And it's a friend you pour out your heart to. So God will pour His heart to you when the sin barrier between you and Him is gone. Would you let sin go?

Every sin that is not repented of is counted against you, it is recorded against your name in heaven. Listen, after all these you've been hearing, if you still accommodate sin, affliction will torture you! Because if God can't get you to return by words, He will do so by His wrath or His rod.

Why is God getting so hot? Because Satan is so mad at your redemption, he wants to bring you down in destruction. But he will not succeed! You must frustrate him. Repent!

God said:

> When I would have healed Israel, then the iniquity of Ephraim was discovered...
>
> Hosea 7:1

Why? It was not repented of. When you repent, He forgives and forgets. When you don't repent, it stands against you in His records.

> ...and the wickedness of Samaria: for they commit falsehood; and the thief cometh in, and the troop of robbers spoileth without.
>
> And they consider not in their hearts that I remember all their wickedness: now their own doings have beset them about; they are before my face.
>
> They make the king glad with their wickedness, and the princes with their lies.
>
> They are all adulterers, as an oven heated by the baker, who ceaseth from raising after he hath kneaded the dough, until it be leavened.
>
> Hosea 7:1-4

When God wanted to do favour, He remembered the unrepented sins, and He withdrew His hand!

Repentance means making a U-turn in the right direction. Let him that steals, steal no more; you may be caught and your shame exposed. Let him that commits adultery do it no more; the next one you do, you may be plagued with an incurable disease! That is why you must be in the Spirit of holiness, to maintain your oath of purity with God.

It's a new day! It's your hour of visitation!

The man Esau turned very late. There was no more

place found for repentance when he eventually repented (Heb. 12:17).

For everything there is a time and a season. Now God is saying: **"Repent! Harden not your heart"**.

If you don't turn now, you may never have another opportunity till Jesus comes. This is your God–given opportunity, you must celebrate it, by applying yourself to it.

It's important for you to turn. God has so harshly and so directly given everyone an opportunity to make his choice. May you make the right choice today!

God said:

> Turn you at my reproof: behold, I will pour out my spirit unto you, I will make known my words unto you.
>
> Proverbs 1:23

He will pour out His Spirit, so that when the enemy comes like a flood, that Spirit will set a standard against him.

God said, **"Turn, and I will give you what it takes not to go back again"**.

## THIS IS THE PATTERN

I want to show you three great scriptures that will provoke you to embrace holiness. This is the pattern for the move of the Spirit.

For the time is come that judgment must begin at the

house of God: and if it first begin at us, what shall the
end be of them that obey not the gospel of God?

1 Peter 4:17

Every move of God follows this order: there is first
conviction. The moment conviction reigns, it goes ahead
to establish righteousness, then judgement strikes!

Nevertheless I tell you the truth; It is expedient for
you that I go away: for if I go not away, the
Comforter will not come unto you; but if I depart,
I will send him unto you.

And when he is come, he will reprove the world of
sin, and of righteousness, and of judgment;

Of sin, because they believe not on me;

Of righteousness, because I go to my Father, and ye
see me no more;

Of judgment, because the prince of this world is
judged.

John 16:7-11

Let's trace the three phases:

He will convict the world of sin...

That's wave number one. That is the Holy Spirit's
regular approach for all the moves of God.

When you refuse to be convicted, you become a

convict! If you let the wave of conviction pass you, you end up as a convict; your destiny is imprisoned!

The foundation of every move of God is conviction of sin. There's a wave of the Spirit on now, bringing about a strong wind of conviction. If you miss it today, you might end up as a convict. But God forbid!

When Jesus met Simon Peter in Luke chapter 5, and that miracle catch took place, Peter said, *"Depart from me, for I am a sinful man!"* With that conviction Jesus' ministry began. Peter was convicted of sin.

When the Holy Ghost came in Acts chapter 2, He began with conviction. After Peter by the Holy Ghost spoke with such power and boldness, the Bible said concerning the people, *"they were pricked in their hearts"*. That is, they were convicted of sin. And 3,000 people gave their lives to Christ!

Of righteousness...

This is the second phase. Conviction brings restoration, and restoration provokes righteousness.

In chapter 2 of Acts, 3,000 people got saved. And in chapter 5, Ananias and Sapphira were killed — to establish righteousness.

...of righteousness, because I go to my Father (having finished the job that I came for, having destroyed him that has the power of sin. Having stripped him naked right inside hell. I am going to my Father, having finished my job. Your struggle against sin I have finished, and I have left you with a choice for righteousness.)

John 16:10 (paraphrased)

And the third phase:

...of judgment, because the prince of this world is judged.

So when conviction has come and righteousness is in place, judgment begins its work, and every work of the devil begins to be humiliated.

When you give room to the first and the second wave, you automatically flow in the third wave—the wave of dominion.

*Of judgement, because the prince of this world is judged already.* That is, whatever you say stands. Whatever you say comes to pass. *"For the Father judgeth no man, but has committed all judgment to the Son".* And as the Father has sent Him, so He has sent us.

Every move of God begins with a wave of conviction. When conviction is concluded, restoration takes over. When you are fully restored to God in righteousness, authority that provokes dominion becomes your possession.

You know conviction began on the day of pentecost. And suddenly, God began to move. The move was going to be corrupted by the tricks of Satan. Then God struck Ananias and Sapphira down!

Judgement began in the house of God. Then fear came upon all men! And in Acts chapter 6, the Word of God increased! That is, revival exploded after the judgement of Ananias and Sapphira. You will not be a specimen of God's judgement!

Judgement is beginning in the house of God! Let him that has ears hear what the Spirit of God is saying to the Church.

The unrighteous will be so humiliated, that others will fear and change! Every move of God comes with judgement, and the judgement begins in the house of God, in order to keep the fire burning.

May you not come out with AIDS from the next immorality you commit, because judgement is beginning in the house of God! May you not find yourself in jail for life for the next thing you steal, because judgement must begin in the house of God!

Friends, the choice is yours!

Every move of God follows these three original phases:

- ➲ The wave of Conviction
- ➲ The wave of Righteousness
- ➲ The wave of Manifestation (because the prince of this world is judged).

Dominion now returns to base — to the sons of

God! When God declares your sonship, your manifestation becomes automatic.

But first, you will have to submit to the law of conviction, the law of righteousness, before you now enter into the law of manifestation.

You need to embrace the law of conviction. Whatever is not right is wrong. Sin does not require any definition. All unrighteousness is sin. Whatever is wrong is sin.

> Bless the Lord, O my soul; and all that is within me, bless his holy name.
>
> Bless the Lord, O my soul, and forget not all his benefits.
>
> Who forgiveth all thine iniquities; who healeth all thy diseases;
>
> Who redeemeth thy life from destruction; who crowneth thee with lovingkindness and tender mercies;
>
> Who satisfieth thy mouth with good things; so that thy youth is renewed like the eagle's
>
> Psalm 103:1-5

It's the same wave. First you are forgiven, then restored and then you're delivered.

His benefits have their foundation in forgiveness. And forgiveness comes by reason of confession, and confession by reason of conviction.

If you're not convicted, you will not confess. If you don't confess you will not be forgiven. If you're not forgiven, you will not be healed — for healing is the children's bread. And when you're out of tune with God, you're no longer a child, you're a dog. Jesus said you don't give the children's bread to dogs (Matt.15:26).

A dog is that which returns to its vomit. Dogs are without. So if you don't get convicted, you will not confess. If you don't confess, you will not be forgiven. If you are not forgiven, you will not be healed. If you're not healed, you will not be delivered. So you remain in slavery!

Friends, I'd like you to open up to the Spirit of holiness. When you allow the Holy Ghost, He pricks your heart for conviction, leading to confession, leading from confession to restoration. So your life can be restored from calamity, from shame, from reproach!

# 3

# Horrors Of Sin!

The soul that sinneth, it shall die.

Ezekiel 18:20

All unrighteousness is sin. Whatever is not right is wrong. Sin brings reproach, it erodes honour, it terminates dignity, it cuts down, it brings low!

At the root of every evil is sin; because before sin came, there was no evil. At the root of every disease is sin. At the root of every frustration is sin. Sin is a spiritual heart disease! And you know that heart disease is the shortest cut to death —"*The soul that sinneth it shall die.*"

The wages of sin is death. It kills joy, finances, the family, peace in the home, the business, etc. That is, you'll be living as a dead man! Because the Bible says, "*He that lives in worldly pleasure is dead while he yet liveth*"—a walking corpse!

The sting of death is sin...

1 Corinthians 15:56

When sin stings, it results in death when not treated on time. If you have a snake bite and it's not treated, you're ready for the grave, because it carries a deadly venom. That's exactly what sin does to the saint. It doesn't matter to the sinner, because he's already dead. Colossians 2:13 says:

And you, being dead in your sins...

The dead can't die anymore, because he's already a dead man, that's his nature. You will not be slain by the traps of sin!

Listen to me, sin will bring such damnations, so as to set fear in the hearts of men. May you not be the specimen that will be used to make others learn a lesson!

The nature of sin is three dimensional:

➲ It is deceptive (Heb. 3:13)

➲ It offers temporal pleasure (Heb. 11:25)

➲ It is destructive! (Pr. 11:3)

You will not be destroyed!

Sin is not a friend of anybody. It is a hideous enemy. It's out with subtlety to disappoint destiny.

Stop it before it stops you! Kill it before it kills you.

Friends, sin is sin, no matter who commits it! Every unrighteousness is sin. Whatever the Bible marks wrong is sin.

Sin is not a friend, it is an enemy! Sin is not a lifter, it is a destroyer! Sin is not a promoter, it is a demoter! Sin does not give people beauty, it makes men ugly!

Listen to this, sin does not require any definition! Whatever is not right is wrong.

Sin is a reproach to any people. Any people means no matter your grade, no matter your category or cadre in life. Today, I see the horror of sin destroyed in your life!

Now, let's look at some of the horrors of sin, the devastating consequences of sin.

## SHAME

Sin is a barrier to honour in anybody's life— white or black, literate or illiterate, young or old. No matter who you are, sin will never allow you to see honour. Wherever sin reigns, shame reigns. Wherever sin reigns, reproach reigns. Wherever sin reigns, men have no future!

You remember when the first man Adam sinned in the garden of Eden? He was stripped naked! God called out to Adam, *"Adam, where art thou?"*

Hear Adam's response in Genesis 3:10:

> ...I heard thy voice in the garden, and I was afraid, because I was NAKED; and I hid myself.

There it is! Sin will strip any man naked of all

honour, dignity and glory! You will not be stripped naked! Adam fell from grace to grass! He became a labourer where he had once been a king.

Friends, sin must die, for your glory to rise!

I want you to know that there is no honour or glory awaiting the crooked. No! He won't get there. Because Proverbs 28:13 warns that:

He that covereth his sins shall not prosper...

Look at this:

For the mystery of iniquity doth already work: only he who now letteth will let, until he be taken out of the way.

2 Thessalonians 2:7

That is, if you don't stop iniquity, it will stop you. If you don't break it, it will break you. If you don't destroy it, it will destroy you!

No one will see glory nor experience honour, as long as he celebrates sin. Integrity is the father of dignity.

Sin will bring shame anytime. The pay day of sin is sure. The earlier you resign from sin, the better! Sin transfers honour from the original owner to another person.

Hear me now therefore, O ye children, and depart not from the words of my mouth.

Remove thy way far from her, and come not nigh the door of her house:

Lest thou give thine honour unto others, and thy years unto the cruel:

Lest strangers be filled with thy wealth; and thy labours be in the house of a stranger;

And thou mourn at the last, when thy flesh and thy body are consumed.

Proverbs 5:7-11

Sin is sin, no matter the colouration! You don't talk of honour where sin reigns. No! Until we get an answer to sin, we will never experience lasting honour.

When the first man, Adam, sinned, he became a struggler, a beggar! He was hiding in holes! Sin stripped him naked! It's time to return.

Isaiah 59:8 says:

The way of peace they know not; and there is no judgment in their goings: they have made them crooked paths; whosoever goeth therein shall not know peace.

Crookedness is a barrier to honour, let it go! If you don't destroy corruption, you will see corruption! When sin is enthroned, shame is inevitable. When sin has its way, honour is lost by the victim.

At the root of every shame is sin. Sin has never

clothed anybody; rather, it strips the gorgeously dressed naked. Adam was clothed in the glory of God, until sin stripped him naked and shame took over. He said, "...*because I was naked; and I hid myself.*"

Sin is the father of shame, while integrity is the father of dignity. You can make your choice.

Everyone that gets married to sin ends up giving birth to children of shame. Every affair with sin ends a man in shame. Sin is a reproach to any people. It is the fastest lane to shame!

Please understand this:

> ...the foundation of God standeth sure, having this seal, The Lord knoweth them that are his. And, Let every one that nameth the name of Christ depart from iniquity.
>
> 2 Timothy 2:19

If you don't depart from iniquity, you'll be humiliated. If you continue to meddle with sin, you will die in shame!

Listen to me, something is happening! God is going to beautify the holy and He's going to "shamify" the sinner. God is going to exalt the righteous, and He's going to bring reproach to the sinner!

# DESTRUCTION!

> The integrity of the upright shall guide them: but the perverseness of transgressors shall destroy them.
>
> Proverbs 11:3

Do you know that behind every trouble of man, at the root of every calamity, is sin? Before sin came, there was no calamity, there was no sickness, no accidents. Before sin came, man was absolutely secure — divine presence was his covering. He was heavenly, gorgeously dressed! It was sin that robbed him of all glory, and he started wearing leaves for clothing! As soon as sin came, all manner of calamities followed, because:

Whoso despiseth the word shall be destroyed...

Proverbs 13:13

If there's a "but" around your life now, it must go; otherwise it will send you packing, just like sin sent Adam packing out of the garden of Eden (Gen. 3:21).

Friends, sin is a destroyer!

Samson was the strength of Israel in the Old Testament, but Satan trapped him! He became a toy for the heathen. He killed more people at his death, but he also died! A mighty treasure turned to a toy overnight.

Sin is a silent killer! It's a destroyer. See how it destroyed the destiny of Samson (Judges 16). It will not destroy your own destiny!

When you see strength, watch out! Satan is out to humiliate it. Everything dies at the hand of sin, because *"the sting of death is sin."*

A young man, an usher, used to steal from the offering bucket. That was his regular source of income. Then he was struck with tuberculosis! When he came and confessed to me, I told him to ask God for mercy. I also pleaded for mercy on his behalf. I desired for him to live, but he died!

Somebody else died, and on his deathbed, he confessed to impropriety of one million naira, which he claimed to have returned. But he died of a horrible disease! *"The sting of death is sin"!*

Watch out friends! God is setting up specimens of destruction. Don't be numbered among them!

The soul that sinneth, it shall die...

God has shown us the path of righteousness so we can destroy the mystery of sin. Let's walk in that path. Enough is enough!

Jesus said to Satan in Luke 4:12:

...Thou shalt not tempt the Lord thy God.

Not everyone that left Egypt arrived Canaan. They did not die a natural death as it were. They died a death of judgement. Not everyone who is born again will arrive Canaan. So let's watch it! It was called the Church in the wilderness. Many died there, they never saw the land. Why? They continued still in sin. They provoked Him to anger, and they were destroyed by the destroyer (1 Cor.10:10)!

You will not be destroyed!

# SICKNESS! DISEASE! AFFLICTIONS!

A sound heart is the life of the flesh: but envy the rottenness of the bones.

Proverbs 14:30

Every disease has its root in sin.

There was no sickness before sin came, no ailment, no cancer. God made provisions for everything in the garden of Eden, but not for healing. Because man was not created to be sick. But by one man sin came, and sin brought death, and everything that leads to death—including leukaemia, cancer, AIDS, name it!

Jesus said to say, *"Thy sins are forgiven thee"*, is the same thing as saying *"arise and be healed"* (Matt. 9:6), because both sin and sickness have the same root.

Every disease is a curse. A curse is as a result of sin (Deut.28:15-68).

. Any sickness—call it fever, chest pain, bad sight, deafness, whatever—the Bible calls them curses. No other theological or medical explanation will be stronger than what the Bible has to say.

Sin is at the root of every disease, and until righteousness takes over, sickness continues!

# ABSENCE OF PEACE

When Israel departed from God and began to do

67

whatever they wanted to, the Bible says that peace departed.

> Now for a long season Israel hath been without the true God, and without a teaching priest, and without law...
>
> And in those times there was no peace to him that went out, nor to him that came in, but great vexations were upon all the inhabitants of the countries.
>
> And nation was destroyed by nation, and city of city: for God did vex them with all adversity.
>
> 2 Chronicles 15:3,5,6

And then the prophet came and began to announce a new order. Just like I'm announcing a new order this hour.

Job 22:21-23 says:

> Acquaint now thyself with him, and be at peace: thereby good shall come unto thee.
>
> Receive, I pray thee, the law from his mouth, and lay up his words in thine heart.
>
> If thou return to the Almighty, thou shalt be built up, thou shalt put away iniquity far from thy tabernacles.

When Asa heard the words of the Prophet Oded, he took steps:

...he took courage, and put away the abominable idols out of all the land of Judah and Benjamin...and renewed the altar of the Lord...

And he gathered all Judah and Benjamin...

And they entered into a covenant to seek the Lord God of their fathers with all their heart and with all their soul.

2 Chronicles 15:8-9,12

And consequently, verses 15 and 19 tell us:

...the Lord gave them rest round about.

And there was no more war unto the five and thirtieth year of the reign of Asa.

I want you to believe God for every seed of the wicked one in you to be destroyed, so that the glory of God in your life can emerge, and the world can see the hand of the Lord upon you.

Before sin finishes you, finish it and enter into your liberty right now!

# 4

# Agents Of Sin

...Stand ye in the ways, and see, and ask for the old paths, where is the good way, and walk therein, and ye shall find rest for your souls. But they said, We will not walk therein.

Jeremiah 6:16

The cheapest way to solving problems is to be accustomed to examples. I've always said you don't have to be intelligent to be a mathematician; just understand the example, and go ahead and use it to solve the problem. If you don't mind examples, you will end up in shambles!

From examples in the scriptures, I located three traps of the enemy against the end-time Church, as stated in 2 Timothy 3:1-5.

This know also, that in the last days perilous times shall come...

In the midst of the glorious hour coming, perilous times will arise for some people. We've been talking about the glorious hour, it's good to also talk about the perilous times. People will earn the glorious hour, and some yet will earn the perilous times.

Verses 2-5 continue:

> For men shall be lovers of their own selves, covetous, boasters, proud, blasphemers, disobedient to parents, unthankful, unholy,

> Without natural affection, trucebreakers, false accusers, incontinent, fierce, despisers of those that are good.

> Traitors, heady, highminded, lovers of pleasures more than lovers of God.

> Having a form of godliness, but denying the power thereof: from such turn away.

These are all the things the enemy will be bringing to defile the saints. You can classify these under three headings:

➲ Immorality

➲ Financial corruption

➲ Rebellion

These are the principal traps by which the enemy is set to destroy great destinies. Yours shall not be destroyed!

## IMMORALITY

Sin is not just sin. Sin is in grades, it's in categories.

When Israel left Egypt and journeyed to the promised land, the highest number that was slain came by sexual immorality. Paul in his writing told us that 23,000 men fell in one day, for fornication (1 Cor. 10:8)! If you check through Bible history, this was the highest rate of calamity throughout their journey from Egypt to Canaan.

Immorality will take its toll among people this endtime. It is therefore important to choose this day, where you will be.

Samson, the strength of Israel in his time, was slain by immorality. He was the treasure of heaven on earth, but he was turned to a toy! He was the gift of God, but became a curse on the earth. All lost to immorality!

Samson lost his throne to a woman. They plucked out his two eyes and made him dance the dance of Israel among the sinners (Judges 16). All by the trap of immorality!

This day must mark the end of sexual sin and immorality in your life!

> For she hath cast down many wounded: yea, many strong men have been slain by her.
>
> Proverbs 7:26

Is that where you want to go? Do you want to be cast down? Do you want to be slain? So watch it!

> Can a man take fire in his bosom, and his clothes not be burned?

Can one go upon hot coals, and his feet not be burned?

So he that goeth in to his neighbour's wife; whosoever toucheth her shall not be innocent.

Proverbs 6:27-29

If you are not innocent, you are condemned. The sin of immorality must go or it will cast you down! Multitudes are waiting for you to manifest; would you give your crown to sin?

And thou mourn at the last, when thy flesh and thy body are consumed.

Proverbs 5:11

The sin of immorality makes you to mourn at last, when the flesh and body are consumed with AIDS, cancer, gonorrhoea, etc.

Samson was reigning by strength, but this strength was cast down by immorality. Sin destroyed the throne of Samson.

...And he awoke out of his sleep, and said, I will go out as at other times before, and shake myself. And he wist not that the Lord was departed from him.

Judges 16:20

So many men are dying as slaves today because sin has not been put under check. It is better to be impotent than to miss heaven to sexual immorality.

It is better to be sexually dead, than to be alive in the flesh and dead in the spirit. It is better to live naked and pave your way to heaven, than to live in a falsified mansion, only to end up in the pit of hell! Why must you destroy your destiny on the laps of Delilah, when the whole earth is waiting for your manifestation?

Listen to me, every time a trumpet is sounding, it's preparing you for what lies ahead. Whatever you saw before was child's play, the one coming now is a vow to kill you. So run!

If you understand examples you can't fail mathematics. You will fail this one if you don't understand the example. Understand the examples and you will be an excellent student.

We have seen how Samson, the strength of Israel, was slain on the laps of Delilah. The beauty of Israel was turned to ashes by sexual immorality!

You remember that giant in Tommy Hicks' prophecy? It rose and cleansed itself from all debris and filth.

1 John 3:3 says:

> And every man that hath this hope in him purifieth himself, even as he is pure.

Friends, there is need for soberness now! There is need for covenant remorse, so that your place will not be lost in this army.

When the Bible says there is a sin unto death, we see that no sin killed more than the sin of fornication in the Church in the wilderness. Twenty three thousand people died in one day—the mercy of God ran out!

Apostle Paul says:

> If any man defile the temple of God, him shall God destroy; for the temple of God is holy, which temple ye are.
>
> 1 Corinthians 3:17

What else is sin unto death? That's why there is an alarm now, saying, "Clean up, time is running out!"

I don't know what sin unto death is, but I know the sin that kills people!

1 Timothy 4:1 talks about seducing spirits:

> Now the Spirit speaketh expressly, that in the latter times some shall depart from the faith, giving heed to seducing spirits, and doctrines of devils.

This endtime, there will be a lot of seduction. Seducing spirits will bring peril to many—spirits that seduce men into immorality. Their hearts will be turned away from God by strange women. They will be carried away from the faith, giving heed to seducing spirits and doctrines of devils. Doctrines of devils boarder on deception, corruption and perversion of scriptures. So, be careful! Be cautious! There is death in the pot!

The next immorality you get into, having heard what you are hearing now, may end up in AIDS, an incurable and destructive disease that kills! So watch it!

·Immorality is a capital sin! It is the most devastating, the most destructive and the most effective in the hand of the devil!

Why? Because it is deceptive, and pleasurable. Concerning Moses, Hebrews 11:25 says he chose *"rather to suffer affliction with the people of God than to enjoy the pleasures of sin for a season."*

Sin is pleasurable, but unfortunately, it is destructive! So awake thou that sleepest and arise from the dead, and Christ will give you light! (Eph. 5:14).

# FINANCIAL CORRUPTION

Another trap of the devil this endtime is that which claimed the second highest number of lives —the sin of financial corruption.

> Then Moses stood in the gate of the camp, and said, Who is on the Lord's side? let him come unto me. And all the sons of Levi gathered themselves together unto him.
>
> And he said unto them, Thus saith the Lord God of Israel, Put every man his sword by his side, and go in and out from gate to gate throughout the camp, and slay every man his brother, and every man his companion, and every man his neighbour.
>
> And the children of Levi did according to the word of Moses: and there fell of the people that day about three thousand men.
>
> Exodus 32:26-28

77

Three thousand men died, holding on to their gold!

> And Moses returned unto the Lord, and said, Oh,
> this people have sinned a great sin, and have made
> them gods of gold.
>
> Exodus 32:31

You remember also the story of Gehazi the servant of Elisha?

> But Gehazi, the servant of Elisha the man of God,
> said, Behold, my master hath spared Naaman this
> Syrian, in not receiving at his hands that which he
> brought: but, as the Lord liveth, I will run after
> him, and take somewhat of him.
>
> So Gehazi followed after Naaman. And when Naaman
> saw him running after him, he lighted down from the
> chariot to meet him, and said, Is all well?
>
> And he said, All is well. My master hath sent me,
> saying, Behold, even now there be come to me
> from mount Ephraim two young men of the sons
> of the prophets; give them, I pray thee, a talent of
> silver, and two changes of garments.
>
> 2 Kings 5:20-22

When he came back from his trip of covetousness, see what happened:

> But he went in, and stood before his master. And
> Elisha said unto him, Whence comest thou, Gehazi?
> And he said, Thy servant went no whither.

And he said unto him, Went not mine heart with thee, when the man turned again from his chariot to meet thee? Is it a time to receive money, and to receive garments, and oliveyards, and vineyards, and sheep, and oxen, and menservants, and maidservants?

The leprosy therefore of Naaman shall cleave unto thee, and unto thy seed for ever. And he went out from his presence a leper as white as snow.

verses 25-27

Friends, why must you carry the leprosy of Naaman, when your destiny is to have twice the unction of Elisha? Why must you let covetousness purchase leprosy for you?

It's over to you! The decision is yours.

# REBELLION

This is another sin that claimed the third largest number of souls in the Church in the wilderness. It claimed an entire household! Look at the account in Numbers 16:

Now Korah, the son of Izhar, the son of Kohath, the son of Levi, and Dathan and Abiram, the sons of Eliab, and On, the son of Peleth, sons of Reuben, took men:

And they rose up before Moses, with certain of the children of Israel, two hundred and fifty princes of the assembly, famous in the congregation, men of renown:

Numbers 16:1-2

They paid for it!

And Moses said, Hereby ye shall know that the Lord hath sent me to do all these works; for I have not done them of mine own mind.

If these men die the common death of all men, or if they be visited after the visitation of all men; then the Lord hath not sent me.

But if the Lord make a new thing, and the earth open her mouth, and swallow them up, with all that appertain unto them, and they go down quick into the pit; then ye shall understand that these men have provoked the Lord.

And it came to pass, as he had made an end of speaking all these words, that the ground clave asunder that was under them:

And the earth opened her mouth, and swallowed them up, and their houses, and all the men that appertained unto Korah, and all their goods.

They, and all that appertained to them, went down alive into the pit, and the earth closed upon them: and they perished from among the congregation.

verses 28-33

And that was how Dathan, Korah and Abiram and 250 others, and all their families perished! Rebellion destroyed an estimated one thousand people in one day! Friends, rebellion is of the devil, don't go for it!

Rebellion is a deliberate reaction against order,

targetted at leadership at all levels in the Church of God. Watch it, it's deadly!

Any church or establishment you find yourself in and you have doubts about the leadership, it is not a place where you can be blessed. So check out of the place, before you're checked out!

Rebellion is a risk! I am telling you this so that you will know the dangers of rebellion. If you reject the order of God, don't expect to survive it.

To wish leadership evil is mental disorder! Heaven is a city of order. Forever, leadership is required for human society to survive — whether in the secular world or in the Church. But if we accept order in the secular, rejecting it in the Church will be playing with fire.

Your thinking ill against any leadership set over you is tearing down your own heritage. And if you have accepted leadership over you in your office, then stop playing with fire rejecting God's order in the Church or in the family.

It is very important to allow order to prevail in your mentality! Rebellion is a costly poison, don't take it!

In any home where divine order is not accepted, peace never reigns. If I may tell you this: the reason my wife enjoys all the goodies from me is because she has never raised an eyebrow against anything I say God told me. You may say, "That is stupid"! Well, it is better to be stupid and be successful, than to be wise and end up a failure (if your wisdom is really wisdom).

Leadership offers direction; it doesn't receive direction from the led. That is why leadership must strive at all levels to hear from God before offering direction to the people. Then anyone who rebels against such direction will pay dearly for it! That was why Dathan, Korah and Abiram died such a strange death.

Exodus 22:28 says:

> Thou shalt not revile the gods, nor curse the ruler of thy people.

Particularly when you are aware of the fact that you will be destroying your own position by doing so.

These times we are in, the Church is going to know such terrific promotions that hell will not be able to sit and fold its hands. Hell will be seeking for who can be pulled down along with it.

That was what happened to Absalom. He set out determinedly to unsit his father David.

> And it came to pass after this, that Absalom prepared him chariots and horses, and fifty men to run before him.

> And Absalom rose up early, and stood beside the way of the gate: and it was so, that when any man that had a controversy came to the king for judgment, then Absalom called unto him, and said, Of what city art thou? And he said, Thy servant is of one of the tribes of Israel.

And Absalom said unto him, See, thy matters are good and right; but there is no man deputed of the king to hear thee.

Absalom said moreover, Oh that I were made judge in the land, that every man which hath any suit or cause might come unto me, and I would do him justice!

And it was so, that when any man came nigh to him to do him obeisance, he put forth his hand, and took him, and kissed him.

And on this manner did Absalom to all Israel that came to the king for judgment: so Absalom stole the hearts of the men of Israel.

2 Samuel 15:1-6

Friends, rebellion is demonic!

Do you know that when Ahithophel (King David's former adviser) gave Absalom counsel on how to kill his father David he rejoiced? (2 Sam. 17:1-4).

But the whole of chapters 15,16,17,18 and 19 of second Samuel tell of the collapse of a rebel! Absalom was the most loved of David's sons. He was destined for the throne. But he lost his destiny to rebellion! Privileged and talented people are the most vulnerable to rebellion.

The Bible says the conspiracy was strong and the people increased continually with Absalom (2 Sam. 15:12). May you never join such demonic increase in any set up you are in! It never pays.

Watch it, every breakaway ministry ends up withered! You cannot disconnect from the root and expect to survive. Ministries can grow from ministries, but it is demonic to be rebellious to get it done!

The Bible tells us in Luke 22:3 that before the rebellion of Judas, Satan entered him. That is why we are warned not to give place to the devil (Eph. 4:27). For instance, you're playing with fire when you allow a man whose ministry you don't believe in to lay hands on you!

Absalom died the death of a scapegoat. We can escape it! It was obvious that Absalom would have been the next king, being king David's first son. In God's agenda, it was there, but he couldn't afford to wait for the time. He must have said, "The way I'm seeing this "youngman" (David), he doesn't want to die yet. When will it be my turn? No! Let's kill him!"

Nobody needs to die for you to rise! There are many stars in the sky, all of them shine. If you're a star, another star shining cannot make you obscure. No! May you enjoy your covenant position in God and await His timings for your liftings, so that you will not crash like Absalom.

Have you ever heard or seen a head-on collision between two birds in the sky? No! The sky is too broad for that to happen. For everything there is a time and a season. For every purpose under the sun there is a time and a season. So, watch it!

In the physical when you're pulling somebody down are you going up? And if you don't stop pulling him down, where do you eventually find yourself? On the floor of course! You will even get to the floor before him. And when he falls, he falls on you! But when you're lifting someone up, where are you going? Up!

When you're pulling any system down, you too are going down! Oh yes! Down! But when you're lifting it up, you go up. Make your choice. I don't see you crashing. So, watch your styles, your approach, your steps, your actions!

Rebellion is a dangerous trap! It will just trap you without you knowing it. It's very subtle! It creeps in on people!

Satan set that subtle trap for Eve and she fell for it! He said to her:

> ...Yea, hath God said, Ye shall not eat of every tree of the garden?
>
> Genesis 3:1

Eve fell for it!

> And when the woman saw that the tree was good for food, and that it was pleasant to the eyes, and a tree to be desired to make one wise, she took of the fruit thereof, and did eat, and gave also unto her husband with·her; and he did eat.
>
> And the eyes of them both were opened, and they knew that they were naked; and they sewed fig leaves together, and made themselves aprons.
>
> verses 6-7

Rebellion is dangerous!

When anybody tries to sell the products of rebellion

85

to you, tell him or her, "I'm wiser! Thank you! Take your product elsewhere".

I have never seen a rebel that made a name. No, not in the Kingdom. The moment you get into rebellion, your name is erased! May God give you understanding!

Ahithophel left his ministry to David and went and joined his rebellious son Absalom, and the Lord turned his counsel to foolishness. Ahithophel ended up hanging himself (2 Sam. 17:23)! Rebellion took him away! He was the brain tank of Israel, but he was joined to rebellion, by the smartness of Absalom.

When they told David that Ahithophel was gone with Absalom, He said:

> Oh Lord, I pray thee, turn the counsel of Ahithophel into foolishness.
>
> I Samuel 15:31

And Ahithophel hanged himself! It wasn't David that hanged him. No! Foolishness overtook him! Rebellion terminated his destiny!

Rebellion always ends one in shame and reproach by the judgement of God that says, "*Thou shalt not suffer a witch to live*" (Ex. 22:18).

1 Samuel 15:23 tells us:

> For rebellion is as the sin of witchcraft...

A witch is not just someone who flies about in the night, looking out for whose blood to suck. God is saying here that no man or woman that is rebellious is permitted to live.

The first rebellion recorded in the Bible was that of Satan in heaven (Isa. 14:12-19) and that is why till now, he is the influence behind every rebellion. It is his ministry.

When you react against leadership, you disqualify yourself from becoming a leader. Rebellion always tells someone, "You can do it better".

In Numbers 12, Miriam and Aaron ganged up against Moses:

> And Miriam and Aaron spake against Moses because of the Ethiopian woman whom he had married: for he had married an Ethiopian woman.
>
> And they said, Hath the Lord indeed spoken only by Moses? hath he not spoken also by us? And the Lord heard it.
>
> Numbers 12:1-2

God reacted!

> And the anger of the Lord was kindled against them; and he departed.
>
> And the cloud departed from off the tabernacle; and, behold, Miriam became leprous, white as snow: and Aaron looked upon Miriam, and, behold, she was leprous.
>
> verses 9-10

Friends, watch it! Rebellion always looks around for who to take. Don't be "takeable"! Watch your statements, let them not be calculated against persons and authority. Stop insinuating opinions! Shut your door against the devil! Don't let him come inside and disrupt your life. Your destiny is in your hand, don't eat it up.

The rebellious will be the greatest victims this endtimes.

I came up with a summation from 2 Timothy 3:1-4:

This know also, that in the last days perilous times shall come.

For men shall be lovers of their own selves, covetous, boasters, proud, blasphemers, disobedient to parents, unthankful, unholy,

Without natural affection, trucebreakers, false accusers, incontinent, fierce, despisers of those that are good.

Traitors, heady, highminded, lovers of pleasures more than lovers of God.

I discovered that all the evil that is mentioned here can be narrowed down, so you can easily get to what they produce. They all culminate in one thing—REBELLION!

It says: "*Lovers of their own selves*"—that's Absalom.

"*Covetous*" — He coveted his father's throne.

"*Boasters*" — He said:

...Oh that I were made judge in the land, that every man which hath any suit or cause might come unto me, and I would do him justice!

2 Samuel 15:4

*"Proud, blasphemers, disobedient to parents"*— He sat at the gate of his father, drawing Israel after himself.

*"Unthankful, unholy, without natural affection..."*— He would go to his father and do obeisance, but it was all hypocrisy. It was mechanical, no natural affection.

And all these culminated in the trap of rebellion, which became his undoing. Listen friends, there's going to be such a release of the spirit of rebellion this endtimes, that people who don't know its naked name will just become its victims.

The moment you begin to react against orders, you are a rebel. It usually doesn't begin on a large scale, it just creeps in unawares! Your boss gives you an instruction for instance, and then you carry it out reluctantly. You're already registering in the school of rebellion!

In 1992, something happened in a certain church in one of our cities. Some fellows in the church rose up against their pastor. One man particularly, was the ringleader. He was raging and ranting, pointing accusing fingers at the pastor.

The pastor said, "Let's be careful, so that what happened to Ananias and Sapphira will not happen here". The man still stood up and began to talk. Right there and then, he slumped and died in the church there! His wife was there and she saw it all happen, so no one would say somebody killed him. He died in rebellion!

Friends, before sin sinks you, sink it!

The end of rebellion is death! Absalom died! Dathan, Korah, and Abiram and their entire household died! Ahithophel died! Judas died!

Now that we are cleaning up, look at all those last days problems—all of them can be interpreted to be rebellion. When you're unthankful, boastful, blasphemous, despiser of those that are good, you are already a rebel.

You have to guard your life against rebellion, because it can come in any form and just creep in on you to destroy you. I've not seen one rebel in the Kingdom who survived. I've not seen one shine as a star on the earth. Every rebel lives grounded. Every one of them!

So it's very, very important for you to be awake! Be alive! Know where you're going and stay on track.

If by any chance you are already caught in the trap of rebellion, withdraw from it now, and free your life.

You see, you don't need to curse a rebel, he's already cursed! Rebellion is simply a rejection of orders —a rejection of instructions. And when you reject instructions, you're set for destruction.

Let's watch it! In the last days, there will be a lot of releases of the spirit of rebellion. It will gather in too many creeping forms. You will not be caught!

There are rebellious wives. And I perceive there are

also rebellious husbands, who don't believe in order. When you don't believe in order, you are a rebel. You may call it reaction, but God calls it rebellion! And He says it is like the sin of witchcraft. So, if you are into rebellion, you're a witch!

Rebellion, as we saw in 1 Samuel 15:23, is equated to witchcraft. And we know that Exodus 22:18 says that no witch is permitted to live. He or she must die! This is not talking about second death. It is judgemental death. The end of rebellion is death.

There's a vivid illustration given in James 1:14-15:

> But every man is tempted, when he is drawn away of his own lust, and enticed.
>
> Then when lust hath conceived, it bringeth forth sin: and sin, when it is finished, bringeth forth death.

That's why I said, before sin finishes you, finish it! Because when sin finishes, death comes. So, don't wait, rebellion is dangerous! None of its victims ever survives.

Instructions are to be obeyed, not to be discussed! The obedient makes the greatest mark in the Kingdom. So go for obedience, and leave rebellion alone. Your opinion is your greatest trap into rebellion. So watch it!

It's also important to know that rebellion is an issue of the heart. It occassionally finds expression through the mouth, but it's actually an issue of the heart.

You see, you don't need to be rebellious for any

reason at all. So take your time and walk in wisdom. When the devil whispers rebellion in your heart, tell him, "Shut up! I know better!"

Hear me again, rebellion is a killer! None of its victims ever survives.

Now, I commend you therefore to God, for a rebellion—free life; a life that jumps at obedience, and is open enough for God to instruct and direct. When that happens, you're going places!

May God give you understanding, so that you will celebrate every instruction that comes as another step up the ladder for you, and celebrate it from your heart. Don't try to look at any instruction objectively. That's dangerous! Look at it obediently, with all the excitement you can stir up in you. Then you are on your way to the top.

# 5

# The Money-Trap

If I have made gold my hope, or have said to the fine gold, Thou art my confidence;

If I rejoice because my wealth was great, and because mine hand had gotten much;

If I beheld the sun when it shined, or the moon walking in brightness;

And my heart hath been secretly enticed, or my mouth hath kissed my hand:

This also were an iniquity to be punished by the judge: for I should have denied the God that is above.

Job 31:24-28

The love of money is the root of all evil. As long as the root is in place, the tree will keep bearing fruits. Until the root is destroyed, there is still hope for the tree.

Let's look at 1 Timothy 6:10:

For the love of money is the root of all evil: which

while some coveted after, they have erred from the faith, and pierced themselves through with many sorrows.

The love of money is the root of all evil, and you give it expression by covetousness. The scripture above says:

Which while some coveted after...

But verse 11 advises:

But thou, O man of God, flee these things; and follow after righteousness, godliness, faith, love, patience, meekness.

Jesus said:

Ye cannot serve God and mammon.

That is, you cannot serve God and money. This makes us know that there are two entities that crave human worship—the Living God and the god of gold. You are either worshipping the Living God or the god of gold. You can't be in the middle.

In Luke 4:5, Satan took Jesus up into a high mountain and showed Him all the kingdom of the world and all the glory thereof, and said to Jesus:

...All this power will I give thee, and the glory of them: for that is delivered unto me; and to whomsoever I will, I give it.

Luke 4:6

Note that Jesus never denied the devil's claim of ownership (in fact, in John 14:30, He referred to him as "the prince of this world"), but said to him:

> ...Get thee behind me, Satan: for it is written, Thou shalt worship the Lord thy God, and him only shalt thou serve.
>
> Luke 4:8

So, for everyone you think is worshipping the devil, it is actually the god of gold he is worshipping. The man in the cult is not there because he likes the devil, he's there because he likes money. All armed robbers are into armed robbery because of money.

The god of gold is the brain behind the afflictions of many. That is why such people end up with all manner of sicknesses and diseases—because the god of gold is a killer god!

You must not be part of it. There's a neater way to make it.

We are here as the light of the world, we should show the world how to do it. We shall not disappoint destiny. God is asking us to clean up, for time is running out. I'd like you to just believe God.

The prophetic ministry of Balaam crashed at the hands of money. The destiny of Gehazi collapsed because of covetousness. Achan's entire household was stoned to death publicly because of covetousness (Joshua 7).

The love of money is the root of all evils. All its

victims end up in sorrow. You will not end your journey in sorrow!

I read the story of a young man who ran to Jesus and asked him:

> ...Good Master, what shall I do that I may inherit eternal life?
>
> Mark 10:17

And Jesus answered:

> Thou knowest the commandments, Do not commit adultery, Do not kill, Do not steal, Do not bear false witness, Defraud not, Honour thy father and mother.
>
> verse 19

And the young man said:

> Master, all these have I observed from my youth.

And Jesus looked at him and loved him! He had no eternal life, he only came to find out how to get it. But with his natural life, he had been able to deal with adultery, falsehood, etc. But this man had a problem — his possession has become his god. He has made a god of gold to himself.

Jesus told him in verse 21:

> ...One thing thou lackest: go thy way, sell whatsoever thou hast, and give to the poor, and thou shalt have treasure in heaven: and come, take up the cross, and follow me.

But the Bible says:

> And he was sad at that saying and went away grieved: for he had great possessions.

Jesus touched his gold!

> ...They that will be rich fall into temptation and a snare, and into many foolish and hurtful lusts, which drown men in destruction and perdition.
>
> 1 Timothy 6:9

Gold is one of the greatest corrupters on this earth! Paul the apostle said, *"The love of money is the root of all evils."* Hear this: your affair with another woman or man is adultery, while your affair with money is idolatory! And the number one commandment says, *"Thou shalt not have any other gods beside me."*

Friends, I want you to watch it! That young man was free from adultery, but he was a victim of idolatory! He preferred the god of gold to eternal life, he *"went away grieved..."* Behind many sorrows on the earth today is money.

When you see a young man looking sad and devastated, the god of gold is afflicting him! He's not sick, his wife is not sick, but his idol (money) is plaguing him with sorrow! Because the love of money naturally invites sorrow.

The eyes are never satisfied with seeing. So every lover of money will always see what he does not have

(Prov. 30:15-16). There's no lover of money who will ever be sorrow-free!

This day, I want you to desperately desire a deliverance from the god of gold. That way, life will add value to you and you will be fresh.

The god of gold is a killer god! Many diseases today have their roots in money.

Remember friends, we are in the days of His power. Gehazi could not connect with power because of the affliction of the god of gold. When he saw that his master rejected the things Naaman offered in return for his healing, he secretly ran after Naaman and said, "My master sent me to you. He just got some guests and he said, I should collect two raiments for them" (2 Kgs. 5:22).

And that was how the god of gold dashed his ministry to the ground. He ended up an established leper, whereas he would have ended up with twice the anointing of Elisha! He lost it! You won't lose your own! Gold will not destroy your destiny!

Those who go after gold miss God, but those who pursue hard after God, will have gold as additions (Matt. 6:33).

We saw how the god of gold trapped and destroyed about 3,000 men, in one day! It blinded them and killed them! (Ex. 32:24-35).

Idolatry is a great sin! To have another god in the place of the Living God is a great sin. Moses cried in Exodus 32:31:

...Oh, this people have sinned a great sin, and have made them gods of gold.

And God vowed to remove their name from His book and in verse 35, we read:

And the Lord plagued the people...

Idolatry is a great sin! It's a great killer sin! And it's a plaguing sin! If you don't count gold as dung, you will become dung! So you must rescue yourself from the god of gold. It's a terrible god!

One of its snaring gifts is covetousness — when nothing you have appeals to you, only what another man has. Take your deliverance from the god of gold today! See how it killed 3,000 people! See how it provoked God to plague His own children!

The love of gold is a killer disease. The Bible calls it the root of all evil. If one evil equals death, then the root of all evil equals all death — death of joy, of peace, progress, health, everything!

Watch it! By the time you get to a position, and then going to church becomes when convenient, or you begin to complain of not having enough time to go to church, you're already on your way! Oh yes! That's the mission of the god of gold — it won't let you keep your covenant relationship with God. May you never see the business expansion that won't let you worship God, in Jesus name!

For what shall it profit a man, if he shall gain the whole world, and lose his own soul?

Mark 8:36

May your name not be removed from the Book of Life for one vain government appointment or contract!

I have told the Lord, "Wherever I will get to and your presence eludes me, let me never get there. Whatever I will own that will make you disown me, may I never own it! Whatever I will possess that will make you dispossess me, let me never possess it! Whatever position I will get to, that I will no longer see you, may I never get there!"

Defile the god of gold today, and say to it: "Get thee hence, get thee behind me you god of gold and silver. I no longer worship you. Get lost!" (Isa. 30:22).

The god of gold is not a friend of anyone.

Isaiah 30:23 promises:

> Then shall he give the rain of thy seed, that thou shalt sow the ground withal; and bread of the increase of the earth, and it shall be fat and plenteous; in that day shall thy cattle feed in large pastures.

That means, when you cast away the god of gold from you, then God will add His own to you. And you know the blessings of the Lord, it maketh rich and addeth no sorrow to it (Prov. 10:22).

When you defile the god of gold, God's own silver and gold is added to you for your beauty. So defile the god of gold today, before it defiles your destiny! Defile the god of gold and then God will beautify you with gold! Defile the god of gold today and you will never see dryness again!

I tell you something, if you're a lover of gold, you can never be free from telling lies. Besides, pride will stick to you like tick to a cloth!

Nebuchadnezzar saw the expansion of his kingdom and he said:

> ...Is not this great Babylon, that I have built for the house of the kingdom by the might of my power, and for the honour of my majesty?
>
> Daniel 4:30

And he was turned to an animal (vs. 33)!

The rich fool in (Lk. 12:16-20) saw his harvest and said, "*My soul rest*". And God said, "*Your body will rest too*"! And that same night he was laid to rest!

When Solomon saw wealth, the spirit of whoredom possessed him! He was King Whoredom—700 wives and 300 concubines (1 Kgs. 11:3)! He was a victim of the god of gold.

It was gold that led Judas to commit suicide — for 30 pieces of silver he sold his Master (Matt. 26:15)! Ananias and Sapphira died by the dagger of the god of gold! Gold killed them. It will not kill you!

Jeshurun (Israel) waxed fat, and then kicked against

**101**

God, and God in turn hid His face from them (Deut. 32:9-25). May God not hide His face from you! They kicked against God in their prosperity. May your prosperity not become your perishing! The covenant prospered them. Then they got trapped by the god of gold. The god of gold brought them down! You will not come down!

What the god of gold does is to bring enemity between you and God.

Know that every time you choose another god, you are inviting God to a wrestling contest. And whoever fought with God and prospered (Job 9:4)?

There is no salvation in gold and silver. Enough of running after it! May every increase you see in your life create an increase in your affection for God! May no increase come your way that will take you away from God!

# HOW DO YOU DEAL WITH THE gOD OF GOLD!

And he said unto them, Take heed, and beware of covetousness: for a man's life consisteth not in the abundance of the things which he possesseth.

Luke 12:15

When you go after the god of gold, you become a fool.

Beware of covetousness!

## Go For Contentment

If any man teach otherwise, and consent not to wholesome words, even the words of our Lord Jesus Christ, and to the doctrine which is according to godliness; He is proud, knowing nothing, but doting about questions and strifes of words, whereof cometh envy, strife, railings, evil surmisings,

Perverse disputings of men of corrupt minds, and destitute of the truth, supposing that gain is godliness: from such withdraw thyself.

But godliness with contentment is great gain.

For we brought nothing into this world, and it is certain we can carry nothing out.

And having food and raiment, let us be therewith content.

1 Timothy 6:3-8

Contentment is the answer to covetousness. Until you are contented, you will remain covetous. Godliness with contentment will lead to the realms of great gain in life. Covetousness is ungodly. It is a sin! It corrupts godliness. But contentment will discipline and subdue it.

Covetousness is one of the major ministries of the god of gold.

Friends, if you can arrest the god of gold, your beauty will emerge from heaven! The moment money is what determines your mood, you're already en-slaved by it!

Look, if money is your reason for seeking God, you'll be disappointed, because the scriptures cannot be broken.

> But they that will be rich fall into temptation and a snare, and into many foolish and hurtful lusts, which drown men in destruction and perdition.
>
> For the love of money is the root of all evil: which while some coveted after, they have erred from the faith, and pierced themselves through with many sorrows.
>
> 1 Timothy 6:9-10

Listen to me, what you have does not determine your value; who you are is what determines your worth!

Your position with God is what determines your ultimate value among men.

I'd like you to be determined in your heart. Subdue covetousness, renew your altar with God. Destroy the altar of financial corruption and stop living for money, so you don't end up as a mourner!

Why am I saying all these? We are in the days of plenty in Zion. The day of His jewels is at hand (Mal. 3:17). His silver and gold are being released to the Church. May it not be our trap!

Job was a man that feared God and eschewed evil, yet he became the greatest in all the east! Job is in heaven now, you too will make it!

Righteousness does not demote, it exalts! But sin is a reproach to anybody. Righteousness is a promoter. Go and tell the truth!

Deal in truth in your businesses and offices! Don't partake in bribery and corruption, it can corrupt your destiny! Don't give it, don't take it! There is a future for you in God!

Don't sware falsely to make money! Tell the truth and you will triumph. Walk straight and your path will be straight. It's a new day for you!

Put your children in the schools you can comfortably afford. The kind of school one goes to is not what determines one's level of intelligence. It is your personal discipline that determines your great future. Be free today!

When you denounce the god of gold, the God of heaven embraces you. And when He embraces you, every discomfort will leave you alone. Because, "*In His presence is fullness of joy and at his right hand, pleasures forever more*" (Ps. 16:11).

God has prophesied your lifting you don't have to be crooked to get it. So, walk straight!

## *Lay Up Treasures In Heaven*

And he spake a parable unto them, saying, The ground of a certain rich man brought forth plentifully:

And he thought within himself, saying, What shall

**105**

I do, because I have no room where to bestow my fruits?

And he said, This will I do: I will pull down my barns, and build greater; and there will I bestow all my fruits and my goods.

And I will say to my soul, Soul, thou hast much goods laid up for many years; take thine ease, eat, drink, and be merry.

But God said unto him, Thou fool, this night thy soul shall be required of thee: then whose shall those things be, which thou hast provided?

So is he that layeth up treasure for himself, and is not rich toward God.

                                           Luke 12:16-21

The key to your freedom from the trap of the god of gold is laying up treasures in heaven. If you stack it up here, you will worship it, because "*where a man's treasure is, there his heart will be* (Matt. 6:21).

But if you lay it up there, it creates a future for you. When God is out of your riches, it becomes risky. When God is kept out of your means, you're already in a pit!

When you're not rich towards God, no matter what you have, you're a poor man! When you have no account with God, no matter where you get to on this earth, you're on the floor! Oh yes!

So the cure to covetousness is the giving life. The

giving life will free you from the trap of the god of gold. Paul was writing in 1 Timothy 6:17:

> Charge them that are rich in this world, that they be not highminded, nor trust in uncertain riches, but in the living God, who giveth us richly all things to enjoy.

This is the cure. The love of money is conquered when you're rich in good works, willing to distribute, ready to let go. And verse 19 adds:

> Laying up in store for themselves a good foundation against the time to come, that they may lay hold on eternal life.

Have you seen the solution now? Every time the Bible points to a problem, it puts the solution by it. Until money becomes like dust to you, God will never let you have it. He said in Job 22:24, "*Then shall you lay up gold as dust...*", not as idol.

When gold is more than dust to you, you will be far from it. God will only allow you to lay it up when it has become dust to you. When it's not dust, He won't let you have it, because you will worship it.

Achan said:

> When I saw among the spoils a goodly Babylonish garment, and two hundred shekels of silver, and a wedge of gold of fifty shekels weight, then I coveted them, and took them; and, behold, they are

hid in the earth in the midst of my tent, and the silver under it.

Joshua 7:21

It was not dust to him, it was an idol. He was sleeping on it, until his sin found him out.

Until money becomes dust to you, God won't let you lay it up. And if you lay it up your own way, you will certainly worship it to your own destruction. But I see a mighty deliverance for you today!

Hear this: lovers of money will never have it. Look at this little poem that God quickened in my heart one day:

## *The "Man" Called Money*

*He is a speed machine*
*No one has ever caught-up with him!*
*Why?*
*He has wings*
*And off in the sky he goes*
*And men are busy running*
*Helter–skelter on the earth*
*To catch-up with him.*
*He soars like an eagle,*
*And men are sweating and swotting on the earth.*
*Watch Him!*
*He is a speed machine*
*An engine that goes in the air*
*No man chases him on earth and catches him.*
*Oh the speed of money!*

*With wings it flies,*
*While those who chase it*
*Remain on the ground.*
*Money is a speed machine.*
*Its chasers are mourners*
*None has ever been satisfied with it.*
*Money has speed*
*Those who chase it don't catch it.*
*But thank God!*
*When you catch God,*
*You have caught good!*

Lovers of money will never have it! And those who get it by crooked means will be killed by it! But the lovers of God will enjoy money automatically.

The love of money is the root of all evils. Everyone who runs after it is always slain by it! Look at that young man we read about in Mark 10. When Jesus touched his "*great possessions*", he decided against eternal life. He went away, saying, as it were, "Take your eternal life, I'll keep my money". His possessions meant much more to him than eternal life did. But a man called Paul the Apostle said:

> ...I count all things but loss for the excellency of the knowledge of Christ Jesus my Lord: for whom I have suffered the loss of all things, and do count them but dung, that I may win Christ.
>
> Philippians 3:8

Because of that, all through his ministry, God gave him plenty of abundance. So much abundance was ministered to him by the saints in various churches. He had all he needed.

## *Be Faithful*

And I say unto you, Make to yourselves friends of the mammon of unrighteousness; that, when ye fail, they may receive you into everlasting habitations.

He that is faithful in that which is least is faithful also in much: and he that is unjust in the least is unjust also in much.

If therefore ye have not been faithful in the unrighteous mammon, who will commit to your trust the true riches?

And if ye have not been faithful in that which is another man's, who shall give you that which is your own?

Luke 16:9-12

The number one way covetousness is expressed is through unfaithfulness. But unfaithfulness will ground you and make you unfruitful!

Unfaithfulness means playing out the other person, with the aim of taking advantage of him. You don't go places that way. From what Jesus said, you're bound to fail. He said, *"that when ye fail..."*

Unfaithfulness guarantees failure in our covenant

walk with God. For instance, you're a driver, and you are given some money to fill the fuel tank, but you then buy half tank and collect receipt for a full tank, because you know no one is likely to check the car to see if that was actually what you bought. You have only succeeded in cutting down your life by half! You have cut down your blessings.

Unfaithfulness is a trap of the devil to make you a failure; don't let him, because God wants to promote you!

Do you know one big error that Jacob made? Before he was born, his destiny had been determined:

> (For the children being not yet born, neither hav-
> ing done any good or evil, that the purpose of God
> according to election might stand, not of works,
> but of him that calleth;)
>
> It was said unto her, The elder shall serve the
> younger.
>
> As it is written, Jacob have I loved, but Esau have
> I hated.
>
> Romans 9:11-13

It was settled even before he was born. So it was the devil that influenced him to supplant his brother (Gen. 27:18-29). He didn't have to do that to be the number one.

He paid for it! He suffered for 14 years under Laban (Gen. 29:18-30). His destiny was tied down for 14 years. For 14 years he languished in the house of Laban, his father–in–law. That is what unfaithfulness can cause a man.

Only repentance got him out of the house of Laban, otherwise he would have died there! He was a slave boy for 14 years—his covenant dignity was swallowed up by unfaithfulness! Let's go for the truth!

The god of gold is the root of all lies, the root of all evils. It expresses itself in unfaithfulness — when a whole man turns to something else, just to lay hold on money. Oh, I've seen many people suffer in the hands of this thing. So watch it!

## *Avoid Debt*

Another way in which covetousness expresses itself is in debt. When you have a flair for owing, you're a victim of covetousness. The moment you have a strong flair for owing, the god of gold has held you captive; because whatever your eyes see; and you long for and you don't have the money for, you will want to borrow to get it. For instance, what is a man borrowing to ride a car for?

The spirit of debt is a terrible one!

The moment you start taking steps that are larger than your own strides, you're cutting down your life without knowing. Let me tell you this: there's always something available, which you can buy with the money you have in your hand.

Whatever I don't have now is not a need, it's a want. And God is committed to meeting my needs according to His riches in glory by Christ Jesus, because I walk in the covenant (Phil. 4:19). There's a size for your present status, all you need is to locate it and be satisfied with it.

Discontentment brings down your speed and makes you defenceless. There's no level where you are now that God has not made provisions for your size of food, house, clothes, etc, so you can be contented and live a happy life.

You remember the parable of Jesus in Matthew 18:23-27? That man couldn't pay his debt, so his creditor commanded that he, his wife, his sons and all that he had be sold, to pay the debt.

You see, no debtor can claim to be comfortable, particularly when in the presence of the one he is owing.

Covetousness on seeing the items says, "why not get it? Go and get it now!" May your taste for debt die today!

In Deuteronomy 28:12, God says:

> ...and thou shalt lend unto many nations, and thou shalt not borrow.

And Paul the apostle re-iterated this in Romans 13:8:

> Owe no man anything...

Borrowing makes you a slave to the lender. That's what Proverbs 22:7 says. And you know Jesus said you can't serve two masters (Matt. 6:24). So if you're a debtor, the one who lent you the money is your number one, your lord. Yet God said, *"Thou shalt have no other gods before me. Thou shalt not make unto thee any graven image, or any likeness of any thing that is in heaven above, or that is in the earth beneath, or that is in the water under the earth. Thou shalt not bow down thyself to them nor serve them..."* (Ex. 20:3,5).

Deuteronomy 15:6 says:

> For the Lord thy God blesseth thee, as he promised thee: and thou shalt lend unto many nations, but thou shalt not borrow; and thou shalt reign over many nations, but they shall not reign over thee.

You don't reign as a debtor; you reign as a creditor, as a lender.

Friends, if you're contented, you will not be trapped by debt. You don't cut your cloth according to your size, you cut it according to your cloth. Now, how can someone be on a salary of 30,000 naira per annum, and be living in a house of 36,000 naira? He's sleeping inside debt! Those who lend you money, are simply lending you money to destroy your destiny!

If you take your stand against debt, you will live! I decided against debt on 4th October 1984 and since then, I've lived debt–free! I got it from Deuteronomy 15:6. If you're a borrower you never see the throne! So sit up! Time is running out! Don't live above your size!

And anyone lending people money to satisfy their

covetousness, know that if you're a waster, God won't bless you.

Listen to me, if you can be free from financial unfaithfulness and the deception of debt, you will live long. Debt is not a way of life. No! What you can't do today, wait till tomorrow. A man's life is not determined by what he has. If you live your size per time, your size will know no limit.

I don't change anything until I have the money for it. Until I have the money I don't even think of it. By the time you borrow to buy a bed, how will you find sleep on it? You have to borrow sleep too!

That thing that borrows in you, I curse it right now!

To borrow money to eat means you're eating beyond your size. To take money from someone to buy shoes means you're wearing shoes bigger than your size. To buy a necklace on hire purchase means you're choking your life. You don't need all that! I see you enter into your freedom right now!

You won't leave debt for your children! When your time on earth is over, it shall be with dignity. The papers of the houses you have built will be at home (at your children's reach), not in the bank. The cars you have, the papers will not be with a finance house, they will be in your house, in Jesus precious name!

The torture of debt should make you fear it. Some have built houses and can't live inside it because of debt. I have seen creditors insult, molest and humiliate their victims. Friends, it's time to be free! May the grace for contentment descend upon your life today and stay on forever!

## Mr. Greed And Mr. Give

Look at this illustrative poem I came up with not long ago:

*I have met two covenant neighbours,*
*Mr Greed and Mr Give.*
*Greed will not give, Give will not greed;*
*Greed is a friend of gold, Give worships God;*
*Greed stores on earth, Give stores in heaven;*
*Greed leads to death, Give leads to life;*
*The choice is mine.*
*I choose Give as my friend;*
*I don't want to end my journey in debt.*
*So help me God.*

You too can make your choice.

When Gehazi ran after greed, he was baptised with leprosy. All manner of diseases are contacted through the love of money—the root of all evils.

Listen to me, if you will allow the covenant to prevail, you will be free from all circumstances of life. Borrowing is ungodly. Wearing clothes on credit is unholy!

Oh, there is a great future for you, Sir! Reach out for it.

Jesus knew no sin, and He knew no lack. The god of

gold had no place in His life, yet He laid up gold as dust. You remember when they needed to feed the 5,000 men in the wilderness? He asked:

Whence shall we buy bread, that these may eat?
John 6:5

The issue was not money, but where to buy bread from, to feed 5,000 men, women and children besides!

It's your turn to swim in covenant fortunes. All you need is to walk clean and refuse financial corruption, refuse the trap of covetousness. Leave unfaithfulness alone and despise debt, then God is committed. Before you knock, the doors will open to you.

It is time to enter into a covenant with God, to destroy the lordship of money over your life. Then you'll begin to see the flow of it beyond your wildest imagination.

Money is not a god, it's a tool. Ecclesiastes 10:19 says, "...*money answereth all things*". So don't let it destroy your life.

Money has destroyed many homes. For instance, there are many homes where the husband is miles away from his wife and children—all because of money! In some cases the man has not seen his children or wife for months, even years! The husband is now in adultery somewhere, the wife is also looking for another husband! Money! Money! Money!

This day ends the rulership of money over your life!

**117**

It shall no longer torment your heart! It shall no longer determine your mood! From this day, your dominion over finances is hereby established! You will never become a victim of the god of gold!

The root is destroyed today. You will be free from every form of evil—no more lying, no more adultery, no more schemings, no more selling of your Christianity to get contracts or jobs. No more! Your family will no longer be under tension! You will not run to another country in search of money, and leave your wife and children behind!

Money will not make you mourn anymore! The cheapest way out is to worship God with it, then you will be free from worshipping it.

When you serve God with your money, you'll never serve sickness with it, nor give your money to hospitals. No! Your entire family will live in divine health. This is God's promise in Exodus 23:25:

> And ye shall serve the Lord your God, and he shall bless thy bread, and thy water; and I will take sickness away from the midst of thee.

From today, this your hand that gives tithes and offerings will never be tight! It will never run dry, in Jesus precious name!

# 6

# You Can Disarm Sin

At the root of every human calamity is sin. Until the root is destroyed the tree will keep bearing fruits. But destroy the root and you've finished the tree!

To every human question, there is an answer in the Bible. God has made adequate provisions to cover all the problems of life.

So the sin question has an absolute answer with Him. When you locate that answer, you step into your freedom.

In the race for righteousness, man is the determining factor, not the devil.

Until the sin question is dealt with, every man's future is in doubt.

You can disarm sin. Oh yes!

How?

# NEW BIRTH

And you, being dead in your sins and the uncircumcision of your flesh, hath he quickened together with him, having forgiven you all trespasses.

Blotting out the handwriting of ordinances that was against us, which was contrary to us, and took it out of the way, nailing it to his cross.

Colossians 2:13-14

Until you're saved, you're not safe!

Please understand that the scriptures cannot be broken. God is no respecter of persons, nor is He a respecter of colour, or connections or age. Until you become a child of God, you're not safe. For:

The soul that sinneth, it shall die!

That's what God's Word says in Ezekiel 18:4.

Until you become a child of God, there's a death sentence hanging over your head! Your education, your status, your age and connections are irrelevant. Until you become a child of God, you will die!

But as many as received him, to them gave he power to become the sons of God, even to them that believe on his name.

John 1:12

God had no business sending Jesus, except for love sake. Would you reject the love of God? Would you frustrate the grace of God?

> For God so loved the world, that he gave his only begotten Son, that whosoever believeth in him should not perish, but have everlasting life.
>
> John 3:16

Friends, it's a new wave altogether! But as many as will open up to Jesus and say, "Jesus, have mercy, forgive me!", will be up! Sin will loose its grip on you instantly!

New birth is the beginning of the adventure into holiness.

If you're too old, too civilized or too smart to accept Jesus as your Lord and Saviour, you can't escape destruction.

For:

> ...Except a man be born again, he cannot see the kingdom of God.
>
> John 3:3

Everything takes its root in righteousness. When the Son of God is received into your life, with all your heart, every other blessing in heaven begins to follow.

Look at it in Psalm 103:2-5

> Bless the Lord, O, my soul, and forget not all his benefits:

Who forgiveth all thine iniquities; who healeth all thy diseases;

Who redeemeth thy life from destruction; who crowneth thee with lovingkindness and tender mercies;

Who satisfieth thy mouth with good things; so that thy youth is renewed like the eagle's.

If it is your choice today to be free from filthiness, there's a blood flowing from Emmanuel's vein, ready to cleanse and sanctify and make you whole.

## SIT DOWN AND THINK

One other treatment for sin is to sit down and think.

...How have I hated instruction, and my heart despised reproof;

And have not obeyed the voice of my teachers, nor inclined mine ear to them that instructed me!

Proverbs 5:12-13

Haggai 1:5 says to you:

Now therefore thus saith the Lord of hosts; Consider your ways.

These facts will help your reasoning:

A wound and dishonour shall he get...

Proverbs 6:33

Now, ask yourself, "Is that what I want to get?" No? Okay, why must you do what will make you get it?"

The Yorubas (West of Nigeria) describe repentance as "Ironu p'iwa da". That is, thinking to effect changes— thinking your way through to positive changes. You remember the story of the prodigal son? He came to a point where he decided to stop and think, and from there his story changed.

> And when he came to himself, he said, How many hired servants of my father's have bread enough and to spare, and I perish with hunger!
>
> Luke 15:17-20

We need to sit down and find out from God's Word, "What benefit can sin offer? What benefit has it ever offered any man?"

The prodigal son reasoned his way back home.

God said in Isaiah 1:18:

> Come now and let us reason together, saith the Lord: though your sins be as scarlet, they shall be as white as snow; though they be red like crimson, they shall be as wool.

If you don't know how to think, you'll never know how to turn.

Stop and think, so you can turn!

This is your hour of restoration!

# EXERCISE YOURSELF

And herein do I exercise myself, to have always a conscience void of offence toward God, and toward men.

Acts 24:16

Christianity is a race, and exercise is the rule of championship in sports. Exercise is what begets exploits.

Nothing goes without force. The kingdom of God suffers violence and only the violent take it by force. Every object assumes a state of rest, until a force is applied. Nothing moves without a force.

When you exercise yourself against any form of unrighteousness, heaven will declare your righteousness. Isaiah 62:2-3 says:

And the Gentiles shall see thy righteousness, and all kings thy glory: and thou shalt be called by a new name, which the mouth of the Lord shall name.

Thou shalt also be a crown of glory in the hand of the Lord, and a royal diadem in the hand of thy God.

You are too dormant to be victorious! Your steps are too weak to be called victorious!

Paul told Timothy:

But refuse profane and old wives' fables, and exercise thyself rather unto godliness.

1 Timothy 4:7

Godliness is established by exercise.

> For bodily exercise profiteth little: but godliness is
> profitable unto all things, having promise of the
> life that now is, and of that which is to come.
>
> 1 Timothy 4:8

Exercise yourself! Exercise yourself unto righteousness. Godliness requires spiritual exercise to be enforced.

It's time to get on the line, so you will not be pushed
out of the way. Godliness is profitable unto all things.
Holiness is the fastest vehicle on earth to anywhere
you desire to get to!

God is calling the Church back to order. Sin is not a
friend of anybody! It is a silent destroyer. It has cast
down many wounded. Many strong men have been
slain by it.

It's time to take your place.

> And every man that striveth for the mastery is
> temperate in all things. Now they do it to obtain
> a corruptible crown; but we an incorruptible.
>
> 1 Corinthians 9:25

And verse 24 says:

> Know ye not that they which run in a race run all, but
> one receiveth the prize? So run, that ye may obtain.

It's a spiritual sport, so it requires exercise.

Paul continued:

**125**

I therefore so run, not as uncertainly; so fight I, not
as one that beateth the air:

But I keep under my body, and bring it into subjection: lest that by any means, when I have preached
to others, I myself should be a castaway.

1 Corinthians 9:26-27

Your body can be subjected by the power of your
will, hooked to the grace of God. To "*keep under*" your
body means to exercise. You say to immorality, "No!"
To bribery and corruption, "No!" You say to your body,
"Shut up there!"

Paul, as anointed as he was, said he had to exercise
himself to the height he found himself.

Exercise yourself against bitterness, envy, strife,
immorality, lying, etc. Bring your body under and say
to your mouth, "Shut up!" Say to your eyes, "Look
here!" That is it!

There is no luck in sports, only those who exercise
excel. If you don't exercise, you fail.

No wrestler enters the ring banking on luck. No!
Otherwise he would be broken into pieces, like spare
parts! No matter what the horoscopes say about you
that day, if you're not used to the punches of a boxer,
and you enter the ring with one, when he hits you,
you will have your teeth and jaw in separate parts!

Boxers exercise Sir! They put some heavy stuff in a sack

and begin to hit it. That's how they exercise. So that when flesh now hits them, it won't break them—their fists are already used to the bruises from the punch bag.

Now, receive strength against the traps of hell!

This is your brightest hour! Your destiny will not crash.

Paul said to Timothy:

> Thou therefore endure hardness, as a good soldier of Jesus Christ.
>
> No man that wareth entangleth himself with the affairs of this life; that he may please him who hath chosen him to be a soldier.
>
> And if a man also strive for masteries, yet is he not crowned, except he strive lawfully.
>
> 2 Timothy 2:3-5

The word "*strive*" connotes exercise. Romans 14:22 says:

> Hast thou faith? have it to thyself before God. Happy is he that condemneth not himself in that thing which he alloweth.

So nothing happens in your life without your permission. When you say, "No!" under God, hell must bow!

Disallow corruption from now. Stand against the arrows of the wicked and the manoeuvrings of hell, for practical holiness, beginning from this day.

In Philippians 3:12-17, Paul said:

> Not as though I had already attained, either were already perfect: but I follow after, if that I may apprehend that for which also I am apprehended of Christ Jesus.

> Brethren, I count not myself to have apprehended: but this one thing I do, forgetting those things which are behind, and reaching forth unto those things which are before,

> I press towards the mark for the prize of the high calling of God in Christ Jesus.

> Let us therefore, as many as be perfect, be thus minded: and if in anything ye be otherwise minded, God shall reveal even this unto you,

> Nevertheless, whereto we have already attained, let us walk by the same rule, let us mind the same thing.

> Brethren, be followers together of me, and mark them which walk so as ye have us for an ensample.

All those are exercises.

Determine in your heart to follow the rules — the law of holiness. Be determined to be like Jesus, to follow until you're like Him.

If Paul pressed, how much more should you. If he was following after, you must be following after. If he was doing something, you must be doing something too, to keep yourself pure.

1 John 3:3 says:

And every man that hath this hope in him purifieth himself, even as he is pure.

Stop waiting for someone to come and do it. You and I must purify ourselves. Godly exercise is the pathway to a dignified Christian life.

Don't wait to see your coffin! Don't watch yourself lying in state. Do something! The prodigal son reasoned his way back home from penury. Paul exercised himself into glory. You too can make your way into glory.

James 1:12-15 have this to say:

Blessed is the man that endureth temptation: for when he is tried, he shall receive the crown of life, which the Lord hath promised to them that love him.

Let no man say when he is tempted, I am tempted of God: for God cannot be tempted with evil, neither tempteth he any man:

But every man is tempted, when he is drawn away of his own lust, and enticed.

Then when lust hath conceived, it bringeth forth sin: and sin, when it is finished, bringeth forth death.

Temptation is a thing to overcome, it's a huddle to cross over.

God tempts no man with evil. Every man is tempted by his own lust (James 1:14). Before sin finishes, let's finish it!

Receive strength for godly exercise from this hour!

Jesus said, "*Watch and pray, that ye enter not into temptation*" (Matt. 26:41).

You must not end your journey a victim of sin! Finish sin today, so it doesn't finish you tomorrow! Finish it! Bring yourself under a covenant oath of purity today.

The horror of sin here on earth is terrible; how do you now imagine what it will be like in hell?

It's time to sit down and think and then brace up for exercise.

Some people are presently sleeping in the wrong places. Get out of there now, before you are flushed out into nakedness and shame! Get out!

Many young people who are yet to be married are in all manner of mess. The home is broken before it started. Then as soon as it begins, it's fighting unlimited, strife and boxing! Because God's hand has been removed!

Stop that sin before it stops you!

# THE WORD ANSWER

For I will take you from among the heathen, and gather you out of all countries, and will bring you into your own land.

Then will I sprinkle clean water upon you, and ye shall be clean: from all your filthiness, and from all your idols, will I cleanse you.

Ezekiel 36:24-25

Ephesians 5:26 also says:

> That he might sanctify and cleanse it with the washing of water by the word.

So that clean water is the clean Word of God.

Jesus said to the disciples in John 15:3:

> Now ye are clean through the word which I have spoken unto you.

God's Word cleanses people.

So if you want to be free from immorality for instance, read Proverbs 5, 6 and 7 and you will be free. It is clean water, it will clean you up.

Psalm 119:9 says:

> Wherewithal shall a young man cleanse his way?
> by taking heed thereto according to thy word.

God's Word cleanses. It washes people clean. So you must exercise yourself in the Word of God that launches a counter attack on the attacks of life.

The Bible says:

> ...When the enemy shall come in like a flood, the Spirit of the Lord shall lift up a standard against him.
>
> Isaiah 59:19

And Psalm 107: 20 tells us:

> He sent his word, and healed them, and delivered them from their destructions.

You will not be destroyed! The mighty hand of God will help you out of the dungeon of hell, in Jesus name.

God's Word is a vital treatment for sin.

> For we wrestle not against flesh and blood, but against principalities, against powers, against the rulers of the darkness of this world, against spiritual wickedness in high places.
>
> Ephesians 6:12

That's what we're contending with. It is rod for rod! The rod of Moses had to be on display, in order for him to be free from the rod of the magicians (Ex. 7:10-12).

It is vow for vow. Goliath vowed to destroy David, David vowed to finish him. And the stronger vow swallowed up the weaker one (1 Sam. 17:43-51).

It is also spirit for spirit. It is the law of the Spirit of life that swallows up the law of sin and death (Rom. 8:2).

God is revealing to us how to disarm wickedness and enjoy our liberty.

We are in the last days. It's a glorious hour for the body of Christ, and a perilous time for the world. But whosoever does not give God His place will join the world in its peril.

You will not join in that, in the name of Jesus.

## GO FOR LIGHT

And then shall the Wicked be revealed, whom the

Lord shall consume with the spirit of his mouth, and shall destroy with the brightness of his coming.

2 Thessalonians 2:8

We are talking about intense revelation, which will disarm the mystery of iniquity. There will be such brightness of light from heaven, revealing the weakness of sin, to establish the triumph of the saints.

We are going to engage the forces of revelation to destroy the strongholds of corruption!

*"The spirit of his mouth and the brightness of his coming"* is talking about revelation, insight, depth.

We are going to be engaging the revelations of the kingdom to disarm the corruptions of hell.

The brightness of His light! The Spirit of His mouth!

There's going to be such an electric effect from the spoken Word, that will liberate totally and completely! Oh yes! The spoken Word will work like wild fire!

We are going to use revelations to counter destructions.

Listen to me, *"My people are destroyed for lack of knowledge"*, says Hosea 4:6; not because the devil is strong in any way. He only hides behind your ignorance to afflict you. But:

The entrance of thy words giveth light; it giveth understanding unto the simple

Psalm 119:130

And this light shines in darkness, and darkness can't handle it (John 1:5)!

So when God's Word is fired into your heart, the struggles end. It ends there, because that light shines in darkness and darkness can't comprehend it.

We are going to punish the devil with the instrument of light!

The night is far spent, the day is nigh, therefore, put on the armour of light, so that darkness will not be able to hang around you. Put on the armour of light, so that integrity can manifest in your life.

Jesus is coming here for a glorious Church, without spot or wrinkle or any such thing. A glorious group of people! So, sin that has slain so many, will be slain in our own time. The devastating effect of sin will become history forever. It will not destroy anymore.

When the Word comes with intense revelation, all the wickedness of the enemy is subdued.

Friends, we've got the answer!

> For the mystery of iniquity doth already work: only he who now letteth will let, until he be taken out of the way.
>
> 2 Thessalonians 2:7

The mystery of iniquity doth already work. So we're going to engage the mystery of Christ to counter it. God will provide such brightness of light that will cheaply disarm the forces of darkness.

He said He will destroy him, *"with the spirit of his mouth and the brightness of his coming"*. That is, God's Word coming forth like fire, destroying all the stubbles and chaff of hell.

# LISTEN TO YOUR CONSCIENCE

Speaking lies in hypocrisy; having their conscience seared with a hot iron.

1 Timothy 4:2

Their conscience is dead!

Paul said in Acts 24:16:

And herein do I exercise myself, to have always a conscience void of offense toward God, and toward men.

Your conscience is the scale of justice. It tells you what is wrong.

That is why nobody will ever come out and say, "I thank God that my woman friend has been so wonderful to me", in the presence of his wife. Nor will anyone say, "I thank God we had a very successful stealing expedition yesterday. We shared 2.4 million, and I have brought my tithe!" Or, "We were in a meeting yesterday, and I lied so much!" No! Nobody says such things. Why? Conscience!

So don't kill your conscience.

> Now the Spirit speaketh expressly, that in the latter times some shall depart from the faith, giving heed to seducing spirits, and doctrines of devils.
>
> 1 Timothy 4:1

Seducing spirits! "It doesn't matter, everybody is doing it". "It's a mistake, it's not sin". Seducing spirits!

Listen to me, sin does not require any definition! Every unrighteousness is sin! Whatever is not right is wrong!

In the last days some will be taken away from God by seducing spirits — the spirits that take men off God, into immorality.

> Speaking lies in hypocrisy, having their conscience seared with hot iron.

No more conscience.

Why? Satan wants to destroy them at the end.

At the beginning, Solomon loved the Lord, (1 Kgs. 3:3). In his later days, it became, *"And Solomon loved many strange women...And his wives turned away his heart* (from the Lord)" (1 Kgs. 11:1,3).

And the Lord was angry with Solomon, and he ended in vanity! Can you see that? *In the last days...*

Oh yes, thank God, we've loved Him, and we're still loving Him. But He's sounding an alarm— "Clean up! Time is running out! The night is far spent! The day is at hand! Put on the armour of light! So you can destroy the manoeuvrings of darkness!"

> This know also, that in the last days perilous times shall come.
>
> 2 Timothy 3:1

So while God is planning glorious times, the devil is planning perilous times, and he wants to see how many he can catch in Zion.

> For men shall be lovers of their own selves...

So there will be a spirit upon the earth that causes men to love the pleasures of sin. That means the enemy will create an affection for sin in the last days. He will increase the taste of men for unchastity, immorality, greed, for anything. Men will run after what is wrong, just to trap whatever pleasure is inside it. All these things are by the spirits unleashed by the enemy.

But you shall not be trapped. Your conscience will be alive, fired up by light from heaven.

## THE POWER OF CHOICE

All through my little life, I have seen the power of choice.

I call it the power that keeps man. I call it the seed of God inside man. I mean, you make your choice and He backs it up, because He is committed to backing it up.

Listen to me, just make the choice against anything you've been doing wrong and that will just end it—particularly as a covenant child, with the blood back-

ing you up. And particularly as Satan legally has no
.ay in your affairs, because Jesus:

> ...hath delivered us from the power of darkness, and
> hath translated us into the kingdom of his dear Son.
>
> Colossians 1:13

And particularly now that sin has no hold on you
anymore, because Colossians 1:14 says:

> In whom we have redemption through his blood,
> even the forgiveness of sins.

And according to Romans 6:14:

> For sin shall not have dominion over you: for ye are
> not under the law, but under grace.

So anybody who chooses liberty can be free.

Even some natural, unregenerated men make some
strong choices and are able to implement them. I read
about a man who would wake up at 2 a.m. (to plan his
day, not to pray, not to read the Bible) and go back to
bed at 5 a.m. That was his natural lifestyle.

I have read so many things about man, that I know
man has such inbuilt power that he doesn't know
much of. It's the power of choice.

When people choose integrity, visitations from heaven
become a regular experience in their lives. If Daniel could
be free by his choice, you can be free too. Look at it:

But Daniel purposed in his heart that he would not
defile himself with the portion of the king's meat,
nor with the wine which he drank: therefore he
requested of the prince of the eunuchs that he
might not defile himself.

Daniel 1:8

If Joseph also could be free by his choice, you can be
free too. We see in Genesis 39:7-9:

And it came to pass after these things, that his
master's wife cast her eyes upon Joseph; and she
said, Lie with me.

But he refused, and said unto his master's wife.
Behold, my master wotteth not what is with me in
the house, and he hath committed all that he hath
to my hand;

There is none greater in this house than I; neither
hath he kept back any thing from me but thee,
because thou art his wife: how then can I do this
great wickedness, and sin against God?

Friends, holiness and purity is a choice to make and
a vision to pursue. It's a covenant life of choice.

In the conflict with sin, your choice is supreme.

Daniel lived in a land of defilement (Babylon)—the
headquarters of sin. But he purposed not to defile
himself. He made a choice for righteousness and
made his way to the throne.

Integrity is the father of dignity. Let's go for it.

**139**

Your choice is supreme in the adventure of righteousness. It is your choice that counts, not the wickedness of Satan.

The prodigal son made a choice one day, and it was effected in his favour. Certain things you are doing now can be stopped, if you stand strong the same way he did, by the power of choice.

It's not the devil, it's your choice! You can make the right choice, and the blood of Jesus will set a seal on it.

From the day the blood of Jesus was shed, sin lost its power. The choice is now left to man. You can't make your choice and the devil thwart it. No!

God is saying:

> Wherefore come out from among them, and be ye separate, saith the Lord, and touch not the unclean thing; and I will receive you,
>
> And will be a Father unto you, and ye shall be my sons and daughters, saith the Lord Almighty.
>
> 2 Corinthians 6:17-18

Come out from among them! Not try to come out. No! Choose to come out! Choose to come out of immorality, lying, financial impropriety, deceptions and craftiness, and choose to be straight.

Choose purity and holiness, and honour will pursue you. Initially it may appear as though you're locked up in a prison (as it was with Joseph), but they will send for you. It may appear as though your business is going down, because you refused to give bribes and kickbacks, but that's when it's rising up, for they will soon send for you. Because:

Righteousness exalts...

When the father of the prodigal son received him back, honour was bestowed on him.

Sin does not give people beauty, it makes ugly! It is salvation that gives beauty. It is just a simple covenant choice you have to make. When that choice is made, you're through!

I see you go through!

I call this the hour of deliverance. Whatever you choose today, in this adventure of holiness, it shall be delivered to you free of charge.

When your choice is made, Satan is finished!

Daniel purposed in his heart not to defile himself and heaven backed him up. You can purpose in your heart now for a sanctified life, which will guarantee a glorified life.

I want you to make a solid decision for holiness. Decide for righteousness!

Make that choice, today!

The job has been completed, God is just waiting for your choice.

...For this purpose the Son of God manifested, that he might destroy the works of the devil.

1 John 3:8

The little foxes, they spoil the vine.

Take us the foxes, the little foxes, that spoil the vines; for our vines have tender grapes.

Song of Solomon 2:15

The little lies, the little malice, the little bitterness—all of that disqualify you for this great army, this glorious army. God is waiting for your choice. You will not be disqualified!

Every sin can be laid aside, every weight can be laid aside. It is your choice that determines what goes on.

The eyes of the Lord run to and fro in all the earth, to show Himself strong in the behalf of them whose hearts are perfect towards Him (2 Chron. 16:9). I want your heart to be straight this hour. And I also want you to understand this: it is your birthright to live the holy life, but it takes your choice to make it a reality.

Sin would have tied down Joseph's destiny in Potiphar's house, but he made a choice for righteousness, and he arrived on the throne in Egypt! You too will arrive on the throne God has set for you.

Where you are is not the best yet, it's only a stepping stone to where you are going. Don't destroy your destiny!

Sin has been destroyed! Make your choice to be free from it!

I see men and women just coming out with bold determination, because when your choice is made, the devil is finished.

The quality of your choice, however, is determined by the quality of information available to you. That's why this book is in your hands.

It's time to flee for your dear life, because fire is burning on the mountain!

Every price you pay to let go of sin, will lead you to a prize in the Kingdom, in the name of Jesus!

## STRENGTH IN THE INNERMAN

Paul was praying in Ephesians 3:14-16:

> For this cause I bow my knees unto the Father of our Lord Jesus Christ;
>
> Of whom the whole family in heaven and earth is named,
>
> That he would grant you, according to the riches of his glory, to be strengthened with might by his Spirit in the inner man.

So that your spirit will stay on its toes in this

holiness adventure. That when you say "No!" heaven will sanction it, that when you say "No!" devils will tremble, that when you say "No!" hell will be crying.

How do we come by strength in the innerman?

When you engage mysteries that are revealed to you, your innerman is being strengthened by them.

If Joseph had fallen into the hands of Potiphar's wife, he would have lost his throne eternally. But there was strength enough in his spirit to say "No!" He fled from the house and landed in the prison, but halleluyah, from the prison to the palace!

Every step you take for righteousness will lead to the throne. No matter the suffering that may come initially, the throne is where you are going.

No matter the price you pay for righteousness, it is not comparable to the prize that God will give to you at the end of the day. So go for righteousness. Let every infidelity, every immorality, corruption, stealing and everything that does not honour Jesus stop today in your life.

Righteousness is your sure foundation for a glorious Christian walk.

Paul continued:

> That Christ may dwell in your hearts by faith: that ye, being rooted and grounded in love,
>
> May be able to comprehend with all saints what is the breadth, and length, and depth, and height;

> And to know the love of Christ, which passeth
> knowledge, that ye might be filled with all the
> fullness of God.
>
> Ephesians 3:17-19

All that come by the strength in your innerman.

So your life and mine are sustained by the state of our spirit–man. When our spirit–man is sick, our body follows suit. When our spirit-man is alive, our physical body is alive. The spirit of a man will sustain him, no matter the attack from hell.

So I want you to engage your spiritman right now, to begin to chart a honourable course for your life. Design honourable habits for your life, the Lord then supplies the grace (Prov.16:9). When it's coming forth from your heart, heaven is committed, because God is looking at the heart.

I want your heart to begin to speak forth holiness and righteousness.

Daniel purposed in his heart, and God supplied the grace. He was under every kind of pressure, but God supplied the grace.

After you gave your life to Christ, no one preached against alcohol, you just discovered it's not befitting for a child of the King, and you gave it up! All you did was purpose in your heart, and God released the strength in your spirit–man.

Right now certain things are going on in your life, that you know if you don't stop them, they will stop you. All you need do is, "Lord, my mind is made up today for a consecrated life; bring me into that realm of honour that You've mapped out for me. I receive strength Lord".

After that, the Bible says, "*Give no place to the devil*" (Eph. 4:27). That is, develop a programme that does not provide opportunities for Satan in your life. Draw up a programme that shuts him out of your schemes.

Daniel purposed in his heart, not with his mouth. He purposed in his heart not to defile himself, and he got through.

Jesus had not shed His blood then, yet sin was rendered helpless. How much more now that the blood that speaketh better things than that of Abel is still flowing from Emmanuel's vein? How much more now that sin no longer has dominion over us?

That was the era of sin, when sin had the final say. Yet the decision of Daniel destroyed the determination of Satan! Daniel purposed in his heart, and that purpose of heart was strong enough to render the devil helpless.

## HOLINESS IS A POSSIBILITY

Heaven is the final home of overcomers. Only overcomers find a place there.

> He that hath an ear, let him hear what the Spirit saith unto the churches; To him that overcometh will I give to eat of the tree of life, which is in the midst of the paradise of God.
>
> Revelations 2:7

You must be determined to overcome sin. The moment you come out with a statement of impossibility, you remain in your captivity till death.

If you see holiness as an impossibility, you die in your sin. The moment you assent that holiness is an impossibility, you remain tied down.

When impossibility is given credence, captivity is enhanced.

Holiness is a possible adventure. To assert it's impossibility is to live in captivity!

When impossibility is given credence to, captivity is enhanced.

If you give expression to impossibility in the journey of holiness, you are already a captive of sin for life!

Heaven is a place for those who have overcome sin.

## STOP THAT HABIT!

Everyone is responsible for his habits. The devil is not responsible for your habits.

> Submit yourselves therefore to God. Resist the devil, and he will flee from you.
>
> James 4:7

Any habit is stoppable, and any new one is formable.

Mike Murdock said, "You don't decide your future; you decide your habits, and your habits decide your future".

It is your habit that creates a habitat. It is your

**147**

attitude that determines your altitude. You can't go any further than the worth of your attitude. It is your character that determines your charisma.

Before that habit stops you, stop it! Before that sin causes you to sink, sink it!

Every bad habit is stoppable. If you don't stop it today, it will stop you tomorrow. If you don't terminate it today, it will terminate your tomorrow.

Paul said:

> And every man that striveth for the mastery is temperate in all things. Now they do it to obtain a corruptible crown; but we an incorruptible.
>
> I therefore so run, not as uncertainly; so fight I, not as one that beateth the air:
>
> But I keep under my body, and bring it into subjection: lest that by any means, when I have preached to others, I myself should be a castaway.
>
> 1 Corinthians 9:25-27

So your body can be brought under subjection. You can tell your mouth, "No more gossip today. I subdue you now, in the name of Jesus!"

You can subdue your taste.

You can subdue the longings of your flesh. Everything about you is "subduable".

Romans 8:12-13 tells us:

Therefore, brethren, we are debtors, not to the flesh, to live after the flesh.

For if ye live after the flesh, ye shall die: but if ye through the Spirit do mortify the deeds of the body, ye shall live.

So we can use the Spirit to mortify the deeds of the flesh, to kill it!

Every habit is according to man's decision. You can decide today to stop that lying, that cheating, those evil thoughts, that covetousness, name it. You can stop it now!

Every time you come up against any habit, enter into a covenant with God on it. Then you have finished the devil completely!

Enter into a covenant with God concerning that habit, you will live in liberty all the days of your life. That is the cheapest access to triumph.

That is it!

# DISCONNECT!

You can disconnect from sin. Jesus said:

Come unto me all ye that labour and are heavy laden, and I will give you rest.

Matthew 11:28

The moment you disconnect from sin, every tree of

evil, of plague and spell that the enemy planted in your body, your family, your business, your finances, will be destroyed. When the root of any tree is destroyed, the life of that tree is gone!

The moment you will to be holy, the root of that tree of sin that is growing in your life (with its attendant fruits of sickness, disease and all manner of plagues) will be destroyed, and the fruits will no more manifest forever! No matter how fresh the tree still looks, it is fake. The root is gone, so the life of that tree is gone!

When you disconnect from sin, all the products of sin die! When you cut off the root from the tree, there's a disconnection — you have destroyed the life of that plant.

Jesus said it in Matthew 15:13, that:

> Every plant, which my heavenly Father hath not planted, shall be rooted up.

He has not planted sin. He said whosoever is born of God does not sin (1 John 3:9), because the seed of God abides in that person.

Now, I want you to disconnect from that sin. Disconnect now! Face it, call it by its name (that sinful habit), say to it, "You have no power over me! I disconnect from you now, by my will, with faith in God!"

Hebrews 12:1 says:

> Wherefore, seeing we also are compassed about

with so great a cloud of witnesses, let us lay aside every weight, and the sin which doth so easily beset us, and let us run with patience the race that is set before us.

This means that we can lay them aside and say, "I'm not doing again". God won't say "*lay aside*", if it's not possible to do so.

The prodigal son laid aside the weight of rebellion, and walked his way back to royalty.

How do you disconnect? Repentance is your disconnection.

Desire is what brings your restoration. And steadfastness will guarantee continuity in your freedom from that sin. Restoration leads to manifestation.

Repentance brought the prodigal son into restoration, and restoration brought him manifestation. He became the envy of the land almost immediately.

See what happened:

But the father said to his servants, Bring forth the best robe, and put it on him; and put a ring on his hand, and shoes on his feet:

And bring hither the fatted calf, and kill it; and let us eat, and be merry.

Luke 15:22-23

When you return, you are going to get speedy honour from heaven.

*Righteousness exalteth a nation, but sin is a reproach to any people* (Prov.14:34). When you are able to locate the cost of sin and the value of righteousness, you will work your way out of sin.

It is my prayer that you won't miss this heaven-sent opportunity to walk out of the dungeon of sin.

Sin will never go on its own. If you don't rise, sin won't go. You can wait from now till eternity; until you rise, sin won't go. Because it's determined to destroy your destiny.

But right now, I see all the forces of filthiness, all the forces of corruption, fleeing from your life forever!

Leave that man! Leave that woman! Leave that illegal business! Leave that corrupt job, before it corrupts your destiny! Righteousness will relocate you. Heaven will find you. Honour will find you!

If you join them in the pleasures of sin, you will also join them in the prize of failure, and in the sufferings of regret!

You will not regret in your life! Your will is stronger than the devil, that is proved from all pages of the scriptures. From this day, sin will not be able to tamper with your destiny, in the name of Jesus!

The former things God has overlooked. He commands everyone, everywhere now, to repent. Disconnect now! This is your hour of restoration.

# ENGAGE THE BLOOD
# WEAPON

There's a brother who was delivered from drug addiction after he read our book, *The Blood Triumph*. He said anytime he was gripped with the urge for drugs, he would say, "The blood of Jesus!", and the taste would die!

Friends, backed up with the blood of the covenant, you become indestructible and insurmountable! You become a threat to the devil. All you need is a genuine choice from the heart.

The blood is our purging mystery. In 1 Corinthians 5:7 Paul said:

> Purge out therefore the old leaven, that ye may be a new lump, as ye are unleavened. For even Christ our passover is sacrificed for us.

When you drink the blood in communion, or sprinkle it or call out to the blood, there is a total purging of everything you present for purging.

The blood of Jesus is the strongest treatment for sin.

The blood of Jesus is our way out of the corruption of sin.

> In whom we have redemption through his blood, the forgiveness of sins, according to the riches of his grace;

Wherein he hath abounded toward us in all wisdom and prudence,

Having made known unto us the mystery of his will, according to his good pleasure which he hath purposed in himself:

*Ephesians 1:7-9*

So we can engage the blood, to bring us into the perfect will of God. He has ordained it that way for us. The blood y is our access into the realms of holiness.

But God commandeth his love toward us, in that, while we were yet sinners, Christ died for us.

Much more then, being now justified by his blood, we shall be saved from wrath through him.

For if, when we were enemies, we were reconciled to God by the death of his Son, much more, being reconciled, we shall be saved by his life.

*Romans 5:8-10*

So we have the answer!

And the blood shall be to you for a token upon the houses where ye are: and when I see the blood, I will pass over you, and the plague shall not be upon you to destroy you, when I smite the land of Egypt.

And ye shall take a bunch of hyssop, and dip it in the blood that is in the bason, and strike the lintel and the two side posts with the blood that is in the bason; and none of you shall go out at the door of his house until the morning.

For the Lord will pass through to smite the Egyptians; and when he seeth the blood upon the lintel, and on the two side posts, the Lord will pass over the door, and will not suffer the destroyer to come in unto your houses to smite you.

And ye shall observe this thing for an ordinance to thee and to thy sons for ever.

Exodus 12:13, 22-24

The passover blood is our stronghold against the corruption of sin. We can engage the blood defence to destroy the corruption of sin. That brother testified of his liberty from drug addiction using the instrument of the blood.

I don't think any other sin is as demonic as drug addiction; it is next to madness! Yet this young man engaged the blood weapon to destroy its hold on him.

The blood is enough defence for you. It's enough to silence the forces of hell. It is enough defence for you in your conflict against sin.

When the taste for sin begins to rise, let your hands be lifted up, as you begin to fight with the blood weaponry. And when you're on your feet, holding the stronghold of the blood in your hand, Satan will know that you are ready for victory, and he will leave you alone.

See what Zechariah 9:11-12 says:

As for thee also, by the blood of thy covenant I have sent forth thy prisoners out of the pit wherein is no water.

Turn you to the strong hold, ye prisoners of hope: even today do I declare that I will render double unto thee.

The universal sin question was solved by the sending forth of the blood of Jesus, because where there is no shedding of blood, there is no remission of sins. The Lamb that was slain,

...hast redeemed us to God, by (His) blood out of every kindred, and tongue, and people and nation.

Revelation 5:9

The blood is the price God paid for your liberty from sin. And that blood is still speaking today.

But ye are come unto mount zion, and unto the city of the living God...and to the blood of sprinkling, that speaketh better things than that of Abel.

Hebrews 12:22, 24

So when you plead that blood, it begins to ring on the Father's table in heaven. Then the angels stand at alert, to deliver, to set free!

This is your hour of liberty!

Neither by the blood of goats and calves, but by his

own blood he entered in once into the holy place, having obtained eternal redemption for us.

For if the blood of bulls and of goats, and the ashes of an heifer sprinkling the unclean; sanctifieth to the purifying of the flesh:

How much more shall the blood of Christ, who through the eternal Spirit offered himself without spot to God, purge your conscience from dead works to serve the living God?

Hebrews 9:12-14

The blood has access to our hearts, for purging.

And for this cause he is the mediator of the new testament, that by means of death, for the redemption of the transgressions that were under the first testament, they which are called might receive the promise of eternal inheritance.

verse 15

The purging preceeds the receiving of the inheritance. That purging is what will lead to our purity; our purity is what will lead to our beauty.

You won't miss your inheritance!

The blood of Jesus will disarm the wickedness of sin and set free whosoever wills.

The blood is our way out.

From today, if it is your desire, (and you can turn that

desire into a covenant with God), if you can hide yourself under the blood for effect, lying, deception, immorality, etc., will all be far away from your habitation.

The blood is the answer to the strongest hold of sin. It has access to your conscience. It can quicken it and bring it back to life, and make you stand on your feet again.

# 7

# Connecting Your Help From Above

For if ye live after the flesh, ye shall die: but if ye through the Spirit do mortify the deeds of the body, ye shall live.

Romans 8:13

In this chapter, I'll be sharing with you on how to kill and destroy the sin nature. We shall be looking at God's prescription for the destruction of the sin nature. The sin nature is a "king", because it issues orders. But when it dies, it has no more power. It has been reigning illegally over your life and your affairs, to damn your destiny, but this time around, we are going to perform its burial ceremony!

When sin is not treated, it kills. When you don't stop it, it stops you! When you don't drop it, it drops you!

When the "king Uzziah" of sin dies in your life, you'll see the Lord. And when you see the Lord, the earth will hear you.

Every bondage is an operation of a spirit.

> For God hath not given us the spirit of fear; but of
> power, and of love, and of a sound mind.
>
> 2 Timothy 1:7

So bondage is by the operation of the spirit of bondage—Satan himself. So it is not what you want, it is what he wants. And to destroy what he wants, we must catch him at the frequency that he operates from.

He is also a spirit, so he operates by spirits. For instance, there's the spirit of fear, the spirit of bondage, unclean spirits. They are all operations and functions of spirits.

But thank God for Romans 8:1-2 that tells us:

> There is therefore now no condemnation to them
> which are in Christ Jesus, who walk not after the
> flesh, but after the Spirit.

> For the law of the Spirit of life in Christ Jesus hath
> made me free from the law of sin and death.

So it is the law of one spirit that subdues the law of another spirit. It is the rod of Moses that swallowed the rods of the magicians. The superior rod will always swallow the lesser one. The superior spirit will swallow the operations of the inferior spirits. The superior law will bring the lesser law under subjection.

So what the law demands is made possible by the

operations of the law of the Spirit. The law on its own is helpless to bring you to a place of sanctity. But when you operate the law of the Spirit, you are able to walk automatically, fulfiling the righteousness of the law.

When you walk in the flesh (i.e when you have only your will and your determination), you don't really have a future. This is because of attacks that may weigh down on your will or your determination.

But there's a higher help.

## THE HOLY SPIRIT

Nevertheless I tell you the truth; It is expedient for you that I go away: for if I go not away, the Comforter will not come unto you; but if I depart, I will send him unto you.

John 16:7

That's a superior helper. When you come to your wits' end, that's where He begins.

True liberty from sin is impossible without the operations of the Spirit of God.

...and where the Spirit of the Lord is, there is liberty.

2 Corinthians 3:17

Zechariah 4:6 says:

...Not by might, nor by power, but by my spirit, saith the Lord of hosts.

**161**

It takes the Holy Spirit to subdue unholy spirits.

Do you know that uncleanliness is a spirit? And what does that unclean spirit do? It brings filth, dirt. That's what it does.

It is law for law, spirit for spirit. So it will take the Holy Spirit to swallow up the unclean spirit.

Moses' rod swallowed the rods of the magicians because he had a superior rod. The unclean spirit has its source in Satan, a fallen angel. While the Holy Spirit has His source in God. And now, we have our source in the exalted Lord of lords and King of kings! To destroy the unclean spirits, you must be operating by the Holy Spirit.

When the devil possesses a man, they say he's now mad, and the man goes about filthy. He no longer knows what it is to take his bath or to comb his hair. He is possessed by an unclean spirit! But when the Holy Spirit comes upon such a man (by the operation of the messengers of God), he discovers he had been unclean.

You need that same Holy Spirit, so that He can swallow up the mysteries of uncleanliness at work in any area of your life.

Remember, He is also the Spirit of holiness. So if you're thirsty for holiness, then go for the Spirit of holiness. For we're not contending with flesh and blood, but with spirits. We can only subdue them by the Spirit. We can only disarm them by the spirit of holiness.

We're confronted by spirits, we can only conquer by

the Spirit. If Moses had no rod in his hand, he would have been slain by the venom coming from the magicians' serpents.

Now, how do you get the Holy Spirit to work, so He can swallow up all the unclean spirits that are out to destroy you with their satanic venom?

## GENUINE THIRST

Ho, every one that thirsteth, come ye to the waters, and he that hath no money; come ye, buy, and eat; yea, come, buy wine and milk without money and without price.

Isaiah 55:1

Are you thirsty for holiness?

Jesus said:

...If any man thirst, let him come unto me, and drink.

He that believeth on me, as the scripture hath said, out of his belly shall flow rivers of living water.

John 7:37-38

This means that it takes a thirst to pull down the Spirit of holiness. You cannot connect His flow without a thirst.

Are you truly thirsty for the flow of holiness? Then go for the flow, for the release of the Spirit of holiness.

For that is your surest security against the wantonness of unclean spirits.

We are in a spiritual conflict, we can't afford to mistake it for natural issues. We are confronted by trenches dug by the enemy, with a determination and an oath to floor us. We need to be spiritually armed. The weapons of our warfare, however, are not carnal, but they are mighty (and spiritual) through God to the pulling down of strongholds.

There's is no true liberty, except by the Spirit; for wherever the Spirit of God is, there is liberty.

Every natural technique can fail, but the Spirit of holiness will never fail in our conflict with sin. So true liberty is the ministry of the Holy Spirit. For by strength shall no man prevail (1 Sam. 2:9).

Be genuinely thirsty for the Spirit of holiness. He will destroy every uprising of sin in your life.

Isaiah 59:19 says:

> So shall they fear the name of the Lord from the west, and his glory from the rising of the sun. When the enemy shall come in like a flood, the Spirit of the Lord shall lift up a standard against him.

So when the enemy is flooding your life with a dogged, devilish, hellish determination to floor you, the Holy Spirit is your only reliable help.

We have always sought to connect with Him for

power, but He also works holiness, so as to enhance the release of power.

Until holiness is worked, the flow of power is dammed. So let's get thirsty for the Holy Spirit and for His ministry of holiness to find total expression in us. And then signs will announce your arrival.

David yearned for it:

O God, thou art my God; early will I seek thee: my soul thirsteth for thee, my flesh longeth for thee in a dry and thirsty land, where no water is;

To see thy power and thy glory, so as I have seen thee in the sanctuary.

Psalm 63:1-2

When heaven sanctions your thirst, your place of security is guaranteed. It's like David was crying, "*In a place where almost no one has a testimony of holiness, in a place that is dry of holiness, dry of your glory, dry of your honour, my soul thirsteth and my flesh longeth for thee. I want to connect with your Spirit, for a difference*".

If you're connected to God and connected to His Holy Spirit, you don't need any human connection on this earth, to climb to the topmost top in your life. He's more than sufficient, He's all you'll ever need.

When you find your help in God, you're helped indeed!

A genuine thirst, a genuine longing, will connect you to the flow of the Spirit of holiness.

There are certain things choking you privately, that only the Holy Spirit can break. Isaiah 10:27 gives us that assurance:

> And it shall come to pass in that day, that his burden shall be taken away from off thy shoulder, and his yoke from off thy neck, and the yoke shall be destroyed because of the anointing.

He's the destroyer of yokes. He's your access to true liberty. He's the key to true holiness. When He takes charge, you can never be floored by the enemy. When He takes charge, He puts you in charge.

The holiness you desire is a product of the Spirit of holiness. So when you thirst for the Spirit of holiness, you have entered into your realm of holiness, because the law of the Spirit goes into operation, to deliver you from the law of sin and death.

If there's no thirst, there's no access. It takes a desire to have an accomplishment. It takes your yearning desperately for the Spirit of holiness, to escape the terrible, mysterious, heavy, "rockety" attack of the enemy against the Church (Rev. 12:12).

Satan has vowed to corrupt the wealth of Zion, we must be fully armed, for we are not fighting against flesh and blood (Eph. 6:12).

> I indeed baptize you with water unto repentance: but he that cometh after me is mightier than I,

whose shoes I am not worthy to bear: he shall baptize you with the Holy Ghost, and with fire.

Whose fan is in his hand, and he will thoroughly purge his floor, and gather his wheat into the garner; but he will burn up the chaff with unquenchable fire.

Matthew 3:11-12

The ministry of the Holy Ghost is principally the ministry of purity. He's the purifying fire. He's the refiner's fire!

## ASK FOR HIM

If ye then, being evil, know how to give good gifts unto your children: how much more shall your heavenly Father give the Holy Spirit to them that ask him?

Luke 11:13

It's not enough to be thirsty, you need to go asking. Zechariah 10:1 says:

Ask ye of the Lord rain in the time of the latter rain; so the Lord shall make bright clouds, and give them showers of rain, to every one grass in the field.

In Acts 4, we were told that the disciples prayed, and the place where they were praying shook, and they were filled with the Holy Ghost, and they spoke God's Word with boldness. They prayed down the Holy Spirit. You must pray down the Spirit of holiness.

**167**

I'd like you to know this: God will give you the Holy Spirit faster than any other thing, if you will just be thirsty for Him, and then express your thirst with a genuine call in prayer.

Until the Holy Spirit takes control, your body remains dead (Rom. 8:13).

Until you call Him by His very name, you never see His holiness at work. He comes to thoroughly purge your system and burn the chaff with an unquenchable fire.

# PRAY IN TONGUES

> But ye, beloved, building up yourselves on your most holy faith, praying in the Holy Ghost.
>
> Jude: 20

Praying in the Holy Ghost is a vital key that is missing in our adventure into holiness.

Praying in the Holy Ghost provides you access into the realms of holiness; because Romans 8:26-28 says:

> Likewise the Spirit also helpeth our infirmities; for we know not what we should pray for as we ought: but the Spirit itself maketh intercession for us with groanings which cannot be uttered.
>
> And he that searcheth the hearts knoweth what is the mind of the Spirit, because he maketh intercession for the saints according to the will of God.
>
> And we know that all things work together for

good to them that love God, to them who are the called according to his purpose.

So, when you're praying in an unknown tongue, you are praying yourself into the centre of His will. And the will of God is that you be clean. That leper came to Jesus and said: *"If thou will, thou canst make me clean"* (Matt. 8:2). And Jesus said to him, *"I will, be thou clean"*.

Sin is a form of leprosy. And just like the physical leprosy separates you from men, this one separates you from God!

Cleanliness is God's will for you. The Holy Ghost prays you into the will of God, for He makes intercessions for the saints, according to the will of God. So, He organises your life to fall in line with the will of God.

God said, *"Be ye holy"*. That's His will. So when you're praying in the Holy Ghost, you pray down the will of God into your life.

1 Corinthians 2:11 tells us that the Holy Ghost knows the mind of God. So, as you pray in tongues, He channels you into the mind of God.

The ultimate height of holiness is attainable by a mysterious law of the Spirit, which is, praying in the Holy Ghost. He helps us pray with unusual access to heaven.

One of the greatest men with the most open testimonies of holiness (Paul the apostle) said:

I thank my God, I speak with tongues more than ye all.

1 Corinthians 14:18

**169**

It's a private gift for your private victory. It's not for public show. It is to chart your course into the will of God.

It's a private and confidential weapon. When you come face to face with an attack of sin, you get into your room, and burst out in tongues and immediately, your taste for that sin is paralysed! Because deliverance answered from heaven as you prayed yourself into the centre of the will of God.

Paul had the brightest testimony of holiness among all the other apostles. Speaking in tongues as we see, was one of his secrets.

Praying in the Holy Ghost is praying in tongues. It's an adventure into the realm of holiness. It keeps you strong in your communication with heaven.

> For he that speaketh in an unknown tongue speaketh not unto men, but unto God: for no man understandeth him; howbeit in the spirit he speaketh mysteries.
>
> 1 Corinthians 14:2

That is, your communication is outside the devil's understanding. He can't connect, so he can't attack! He doesn't know what you're talking about.

When you're tuned to the Spirit, everything gives way to you on the earth.

As you're praying or speaking in tongues, the fire of

the Holy Ghost begins to work inside your body, to burn off all the chaff and purify you for the Lord's coming. This is one of the ways to purify yourself as He said in 1 John 3:3.

When you operate the law of the Spirit, you destroy the operations of the law of the spirit of sin and death.

So these three laws:

➲ Be thirsty

➲ Ask

➲ Pray in tongues

will help you to mortify the deeds of the flesh anytime.

# 8

# Some Effective Prescriptions

I want to deliver to you two prescriptions by the Holy Ghost, that will help you sail through safely in this end-time. They will put you on the solid rock the remaining days of your life.

If immorality, infidelity and unchastity are the devil's plan for this hour, we must look out for scriptural solutions to destroy them.

## THE POWER OF YOUR WILL

One of the waves of the endtime is the willingness of the people. Psalm 110:3 says, *"Thy people shall be willing in the day of thy power."*

WILLING!!!

I saw something amazing in Mark 10:

> And when he was gone forth into the way, there came one running, and kneeled to him, and asked

him, Good Master, what shall I do that I may inherit eternal life?

And Jesus said unto him, Why callest thou me good? there is none good but one, that is, God.

Thou knowest the commandments, Do not commit adultery, Do not kill, Do not steal, Do not bear false witness, Defraud not, Honour thy father and mother.

And he answered and said unto him, Master, all these have I observed from my youth.

Then Jesus beholding him loved him, and said unto him, One thing thou lackest: go thy way, sell whatsoever thou hast, and give to the poor, and thou shalt have treasure in heaven: and come, take up the cross, and follow me.

And he was sad at that saying, and went away grieved: for he had great possessions.

And Jesus looked round about, and saith unto his disciples, How hardly shall they that have riches enter into the kingdom of God!

Mark 10:17-23

Verse 20 startled me. This man had no eternal life remember, all he had was the human life. But look at what he said:

...Master, all these have I observed from my youth.

This man came to look for eternal life, he didn't have it yet.

Then Jesus beholding him, loved him,

That means he told the truth. He had no eternal life, yet he had observed sanctity from his youth— he had command over adultery, murder, fraud— he could not be corrupted by them.

All these have I observed from my youth.

By what means? By the means of his will!

Your will is a force of deliverance, a force of liberty.

This man, with his "inferior" life (as compared to our superior, eternal life) was able to handle stealing, fraud, falsehood, etc, and Jesus loved him!

His will was responsible for that level of sanctity.

The will is a potent heaven–invested force inside every mortal being. It is a God–given force for man's liberty. It is able to determine your habits.

What you want is a desire, what you will is a decision.

Your desire may be dislodged, but your decision is stronger than your desire.

"I don't want to!" That's okay. Now, what is your decision? We have heard what you don't want, now what do you want? What is your decision, based on what you don't want?

That man came looking for eternal life, but even before he found it, his will had kept him in charge. Daniel purposed in his heart, he decided inside himself not to defile himself. Not even the den of lions could cause that decision to waver. He was ready to be held in captivity for life, rather than defile himself (Dan. 1:8).

In Genesis 39:9, Joseph said, *"How can I do this thing and sin against God?"*

Friends, the will of man is supreme in the contest with sin.

Your desire is your wish, your decision is your choice.

God said in Deuteronomy 30:19, *"I lay before you life and death. Choose life that ye may live"*.

Your will is your choice, because your will is your decision.

He said, *"Choose life that you shall live"*. So whatever you will is a force on this earth.

Jesus said, *"Whosoever will, let him come..."* That means, no devil can stop you from coming, if you will. He didn't say, "Let him pray", He said, *"Whosoever will, let him come and drink of the water of life freely. Whosoever wills to come, I will in no wise cast out"* (John 6:37).

So your will is what initiates His will. Draw near to God and He will draw near to you. So, it is your will that determines His will.

Therefore, if you will for purity today, no spirit of filthiness can prevail against your will.

That man came to ask for the way of eternal life. You already have eternal life. He had only human life, yet he overcame the spirit of adultery, murder, falsehood, fraud, rebellion and he honoured his father and his mother from his youth. Now, you have eternal life. Don't let God be angry with you.

It is your will that determines your way. Until you will, you don't win.

Your will is your determination and the expression of your decision. And that determines your destination.

Until you will, you don't win.

Your will is supreme in your contest with sin any day! It is your will that wheels you on.

It is important for you to know that you have a will and that your will is strong enough to destroy every attack that is arrayed against your destiny.

If Joseph's will prevailed, your will will prevail against the forces and holocaust of immorality too! If the will of Daniel prevailed against defilement, your will will prevail against every attack of defilement in your life.

It's time to engage your will. It is a potent force invested and deposited in you, for your purity, your victory, and your conquest in life.

So engage your will to establish your destiny. Make known your decision, both to heaven and to hell— that you will stand on your feet and see victory every day of your life.

Your will determines your tomorrow. Cleansing is an act of the will, buttressed with the violence of faith.

I saw one very great prophetic parable in Hebrews 9:16-17:

> For where a testament is, there must also of necessity be the death of the testator.

> For a testament is of force after men are dead: otherwise it is of no strength at all while the testator liveth.

Is that not true?

Somebody writes something down, but it is not operated upon until after his death. Because as long as he is alive, he is still the owner of all those things he willed out on paper. The testament is a document that becomes operational only after the death of the testator.

Now, how does that apply to you and me?

Paul said in Colossians 3:3:

> For ye are dead, and your life is hid with Christ in God.

So, you are a dead man now! So your will is in force on this earth today! You were crucified with Christ. Though you are still living, the life you now live, you are living by the faith of the Son of God, who died for you and gave Himself for you.

Because you are dead, your will is in force. You are legally covered to will anything you will. When it is your will, the way will be clear.

So God is waiting for your decision. Your decision will compel your determination. And your determination will determine your destination.

If your will is not in place in your contest with sin, you will be a victim.

Everything you want is a mere desire, it is a wish. But everything you will becomes a decision, and compels determination. Daniel determined, he won. Joseph willed, he won. The young man who met Jesus willed, he conquered. If you will, you win!

These are serious survival strategies. You need to be able to hold them tightly in your hand. When you say "No!" and mean it, it becomes a will.

Friends, you have the gift of your will from God, engage it, beginning from now, for your liberty on this earth.

If it is your will to stop beating your wife, for instance, there's no way your hand will ever go up to hit her again. It has been your wish all the while, that's why you are washed out. But when it becomes your will, Satan will give up. When your choice is made, Satan is finished!

If you will total, endless liberty from immorality, it will be enforced and sanctioned in heaven and bowed to by hell. Why? You are a "dead" testator, your will is enforced by law.

If it is your will to devastate the trap of sin this endtime, that will is in force, and heaven will back it up.

So God is waiting for you, to see which way you're going. Without a will, you have no way out! Your will is your strength in the contest with sin. Your will is your greatest resistance in the contest with sin.

If you miss heaven at the end of your journey, you are of all men most miserable. If the gate of heaven refuses to open to you when you leave here, then you have wasted a whole lifetime! But God forbid! So let your will be in force now.

"If you will, I will", that's what Jesus is saying.

It's time to say,

**"I will for purity!**

**I will for holiness!**

**I will for righteousness!**

**I will against sin!**

**I will against immorality**

**I will against strife!**

**I will against distractions!**

**I will against stealing!**

**I will against lying."**

Your will determines God's will for you. May your will be properly in place this endtime, against the onslaught of Satan. Oh yes, he's out with a vow, we must destroy him with a stronger vow.

Do you will to be holy?

Every accomplishment begins with a desire. When

your desire becomes a hearty desire, every gate of hell crumbles at your appearance.

If it is your will to be clean, the taste for sin will die now!

Shadrach, Meshach and Abednego saw the fiery furnace, but their will never bowed. Daniel saw the den of lions, his will didn't crumble.

Oh, the will is a potent force! When engaged in the covenant, you become unbeatable.

If the will of man is stronger than sin, how much more the will of God Who said, "*Be ye holy for I am holy*". He's the same God that said, "*Let there be light!*" *and there was light.* So if He says, "*Be ye holy*", it is because you have all it takes to be holy, if you want to be.

The moment your choice is made, Satan is finished! That young man said to Jesus, "*All these have I observed from my youth*".

Listen friends, 20 years from now, your testimony of holiness will remain strong and ever strong! Your testimony of righteousness will be established, and heaven will take notice of you. A quick work will the Lord your God do!

This is your hour of visitation, don't toy with it!

## TAKE AN OATH FOR PURITY

So she caught him, and kissed him, and with an impudent face said unto him,

**181**

I have peace offerings with me; this day have I payed my vows.

Therefore came I forth to meet thee, diligently to seek thy face, and I have found thee.

Proverbs 7:13-15

This scripture is talking about the adventure of adultery. It was an adventure of vows.

Satan has vowed to cast you down, you too must vow to destroy him, and free yourself! It is rod for rod, a tooth for a tooth and an eye for an eye. It is law for law.

If Satan has vowed, you cannot be jesting! Goliath vowed to destroy David, David vowed to destroy him too. The stronger vow swallowed the lesser one.

Goliath swore in the name of his gods, David swore in the name of His God:

...Thou comest to me with a sword, and with a spear, and with a shield: but I come to thee in the name of the Lord of hosts, the God of the armies of Israel, whom thou hast defied.

1 Samuel 17:45

If David was just talking, Goliath would have mashed him and eaten his flesh!

Satan has vowed, are you jesting? He has taken a blood oath, but his blood is the blood of bulls and calves. When you now take a Jesus blood oath, it will swallow up his own oath as though it never existed.

Satan has vowed! You and I must counter his vow by our own vows.

We are going to punish the devil and all his demons!

It is time to counter satanic vows with covenant vows. When you enter into an oath with God, it is called a covenant. And every covenant that is ratified by the blood of Jesus is supreme, because that is the blood of the everlasting covenant. Forever, that blood covers any covenant you make.

To maintain purity, sanctity and holiness forever, you need a vow; if you will not be floored.

When attacks came on me at the onset of the ministry, from so called well–wishers, I didn't argue with them. Satan was determined to stop me, so I determined to stop him, by countering him with an oath. I said, "God, should I pretend not to have heard you, see to it that I don't succeed in any other thing I do!" After that, everything anybody said was just by the way. I was under an oath!

What an oath does is to establish your steadfastness to your will; it puts it on your choice, and ends all strife. That's why till tomorrow, I don't have any alternative, I don't have any distraction, I am under an oath. I have not dared to invest a dime in any other business since I came into ministry. Because it will not succeed—I am under an oath!

Paul said, "*Woe is me if I preach not the gospel*".

He put himself under an oath. So all the upsetting situations all around him didn't bother him at all! He was under a covenant oath with God.

When you come under a covenant oath for purity, your life will become a challenge even to yourself!

Let's look at Hebrews 6:13 and 16

> For when God made promise to Abraham, because he could swear by no greater, he sware by himself.

> For men verily swear by the greater: and an oath for confirmation is to them an end of all strife.

Your struggle with sin will end when you enter into an oath for confirmation.

Verse 17:

> Wherein God, willing more abundantly to shew unto the heirs to promise the immutability of his counsel, confirmed it by an oath.

That means God sanctions the strategy of oaths.

Verse 18:

> That by two immutable things, in which it was impossible for God to lie, we might have a strong consolation, who have fled for refuge to lay hold upon the hope set before us.

So an oath brings a strong consolation and guarantees your destination, so you don't miss the hope set before you.

I'd like you to know that Satan is not playing. He's all out!

When my wife and I were in courtship, Satan whispered to me, "I will make sure you fall!" I said to him, "Satan, you're too small!" And I said to God, "If I ever do it, put leprosy on me!" That ended the strife!

Do you want to get to where you're going? Understand the mystery of oaths. An oath seals a confirmation of your decision. When you get into an oath for purity, it refrains you.

Friends, Satan is swearing, you can't just be speaking! Satan is swearing, you can't just be making fun! If you don't swear, he will sweep you off your destiny! Look at Proverbs 7:13-14 again:

> So she caught him, and kissed him, and with an impudent face said unto him,

> I have peace offerings with me; this day have I payed my vows.

Immorality has vowed to ruin the Church! Immorality has vowed to devastate the strength of Zion! There must be a counter vow to swallow up that vow.

Satan has sworn, so you have to swear, to swallow up his own oath. Satan has vowed your destruction, you must vow his devastation him!

Hitherto, the Church has been satisfied with praying and fasting. But those are not fundamental issues, they are all in the conclusions. These things you're hearing now are the foundations that will help your prayers to go up like lightening .

Your will and your oath will put you over any demonic attack any day, anytime. So let your desire graduate to a decision. Let your decision graduate to a confirmation—confirmation is an oath.

We are going to punish the devil! Oh yes! Sin is going to lose market. So all the consequences of sin will have no more victims.

God has determined to punish the devil by us! You must join in this mighty move of God.

The moment you enter into the realm of oath, you've come to the end of struggles.

When you enter the oath realm in your conflict with sin, you have ended the strife! The match is over!

Ah! We are going to punish the devil! An oath constitutes a strong assurance that you won't miss your place in this mighty move of God.

An oath brings steadfastness. It compels continuity. It keeps you on the move.

God bound Himself by an oath to Israel. That is why inspite of all the evil they were doing, He couldn't punish them. He will always remember the oath He made to Abraham, and would restrain Himself.

An oath restrains men from being victims of evil.

Till today, that oath of faith I made when I came into ministry has kept my eyes single. I've never looked anywhere else. I've remained on my job, and it shows!

Look, there's no cheaper way to weaken the devil! Only an oath will confirm your state and establish your destiny.

We are training up to be in the forefront of this great army that is emerging in this end-time, so we can become members of the assault company— where we will humiliate the devil and punish him who has punished humanity to this time.

The only way to enlist in that army is to come under an oath for purity.

We have had too many sin analysts, God is now sending to us sin "solutionists", people who have serious survival strategies (delivered to them by God) to offer.

God said to me, "*The hour has come to liberate the world from all oppressions of the devil*". That's the only mission this ministry has.

Sin is one of Satan's most terrible oppressions. More than 80% of the AIDS in town is transmitted by sin. Diseases that are transmitted by the sin of immorality are countless! When you capture the devil at the sin level, you have rooted him out.

Hear this: your will is a force to reckon with in the

contest with sin. And an oath is a confirmation that the end of struggles has come.

Jesus loved righteousness and hated wickedness, therefore God exalted Him, and anointed Him with the oil of gladness above all His fellows (Ps. 45:7). I'd like you to express your will to God and express it to the devil as well!

Until you will, you don't win. The will is what is commonly called determination. It is determination that determines destination.

I see you punish the devil with a new lifestyle!

God is mustering an army, you will not be counted unworthy! I'd like you to believe God for grace to enter into the oath realm in your quest for purity. There is no attack from hell that can dislodge a covenant oath with God—not even death staring you in the face! You remember Daniel? You remember Shadrach, Meshach and Abednego? An oath is the end of all strife.

If you don't vow, you will be floored. Satan has vowed to kill you, you must vow to live!

You need to bring yourself under a covenant oath for survival in this great hour of crisis.

Heaven is sweeter sir! I mustn't miss it. I am doggedly determined to get there — to the place that has been prepared for me.

It's left to you! Have nothing to do with lies!

Nothing to do with deceptions! Nothing to do with immorality! Nothing to do with pride! It's time to walk straight with God. You can counter any vow from hell. Your vow is your strength in the hour of crisis. In the day of conflict, your covenant oath is your strongest strength.

Sin is a spiritual object and a weight. It requires a force to move. Every object assumes a state of rest until a force is applied to it.

I'm glad to let you know that every weight of sin is "layable". The Bible say, *"Lay aside every weight and every sin..."*

I want you to bring yourself under an oath — a covenant oath for purity. Holiness is a possibility.

Sin is not your Lord. Your natural will is stronger than it. Your covenant oath will destroy it forever! We've seen how others were set free, so you too can be free if you so choose. God has shown us the weakness of sin and how to deal with it. Have a will, and bring yourself under a covenant oath.

Until your will is in place, an oath is a risk. But when your will is in place, an oath becomes your security.

The sting of sin is death. But thanks be to God, who has abolished both in Christ Jesus.

If you will, God will. Your will will pave the way. Until you will, you don't win. Will and Win!

# 9

# Rewards Of Righteousness

Righteousness exalteth a nation: but sin is a reproach to any people.

Proverbs 14:34

Sin brings a curse; righteousness brings blessings.

Psalm 112:1-3 tells us:

Praise ye the Lord. Blessed is the man that feareth the Lord, that delighteth greatly in his commandments.

His seed shall be mighty upon earth: the generation of the upright shall be blessed.

Wealth and riches shall be in his house: and his righteousness endureth for ever.

Everywhere you see God blessing, righteousness is in place.

While the wages of sin is death, the wages of righteousness is life more abundant. There is a lot more pleasure in righteousness than there is in sin.

# PROSPERITY! PROMOTIONS! HONOUR!

But my horn shalt thou exalt like the horn of an unicorn: I shall be anointed with fresh oil.

Mine eye also shall see my desire on mine enemies, and mine ears shall hear my desire of the wicked that rise up against me.

The righteous shall flourish like the palm tree: he shall grow like a cedar in Lebanon.

Those that be planted in the house of the Lord shall flourish in the courts of our God.

They shall still bring forth fruit in old age; they shall be fat and flourishing.

Psalm 92:10-14

No matter the drought, the righteous shall flourish, his leaves will remain green.

Job flourished by righteousness, everyone that practises righteousness, will flourish the same way.

There was a man in the land of Uz, whose name was Job; and that man was perfect and upright, and one that feared God, and eschewed evil.

> And there were born unto him seven sons and three daughters.
>
> His substance also was seven thousand sheep, and three thousand camels, and five hundred she asses, and a very great household; so that this man was the greatest of all the men of the east.
>
> Job 1:1-3

Righteousness was the root of the height that Job got to.

Evil must die in your life, so that the glory that God has mapped out for you will come out.

Job became the greatest man; not through crookedness nor perverseness, but through uprightness and godly perfection.

He was scared of evil, he never touched it. He never played with it. Look at Job 1:5

> And it was so, when the days of their feasting were gone about, that Job sent and sanctified them, and rose up early in the morning, and offered burnt offerings according to the number of them all: for Job said, It may be that my sons have sinned, and cursed God in their hearts. Thus did Job continually.

That he avoided evil suggests that he was living in the days of evil. But he never partook of it. Yet he became the greatest man in the east! You will not sell your birthright for a morsel of meat!

Righteousness announces promotions for the righteous.

Who is righteous? Whosoever doeth righteousness. Joseph fled from sin! His trouble became his triumph. The prison yard became his palace. Even in the prison, he prospered!

Righteousness holds a guarantee for your prosperity. That prodigal son said, "*I will arise and go!*" And he arose and went. And every devil was looking at him go. He walked his way back into liberty and honour.

It's time to get back into honour. All the righteous I read about in my Bible were honoured.

Potiphar's wife would have ended Joseph's ministry as a steward, but righteousness paved his way to the throne.

The king's rich food would have defiled Daniel and made him just a civil servant in that country, but righteousness exalted him. He wouldn't deny his God. No! Not even in the face of death! He walked gallantly into the den of lions, and righteousness preserved him (Prov. 11:3)! He ended up in the high places of the government of his time!

Honour has its root in righteousness.

See what Daniel 12:3 tells us:

And they that be wise shall shine as the brightness of the firmament; and they that turn many to righteousness, as the stars for ever and ever.

So righteousness causes men to shine as stars. Oh yes!

If you truly desire honour, then wisdom demands that you also desire righteousness with a greater intensity. Let your desire for righteousness be more than your desire for honour. When righteousness is in place, honour is automatic.

All who stood for God in the scriptures, God stood by them! Daniel would not defile himself, God made him the king of the land. Joseph would not touch Potiphar's wife, God made him a king and a ruler in the land.

Friends, honour is guaranteed when practical righteousness is in place! Desire righteousness, honour will follow suit. It is automatic!

No matter how many principles you put together, until righteousness takes its place, honour is not in view. Righteousness is the root of honour. When it's out of place, honour is out of the question.

Holiness is the cheapest way to the topmost top. You don't need to be crooked to become great. No! Job was a perfect man, he became the greatest in all the east.

You don't need financial perversion or immorality to gain access to the throne. Whatever throne unrighteousness places you on, it is so it can bring you to utter shame at the end. Don't do it!

Listen, there shall be such magnetic, enviable liftings coming into the Church on the pedestal of holiness! We're on the lookout for testimonies of deliverances from corruption in these days we're in.

Friends, "*Righteousness exalts, but sin is a reproach to any people*". Until we get out of sin, honour is not in view.

Every accomplishment in the Kingdom is borne of a desire. The lack of desire for righteousness is the reason for the captivity of sin. Where there's no desire, there's no accomplishment (Mark 11:24).

I want you to be wise. Since honour is an offspring of righteousness, then desire righteousness. Honour will locate you if you make your choice for righteousness and holiness.

The eyes of the Lord run to and fro through all the earth, to show Himself strong on behalf of anyone whose heart is perfect towards Him. So, God's eyes can enter any prison and pick up any man. God's eyes found Joseph. While he was in prison, God was organising promotion for him. Pharaoh in his dilemma asked:

> ...Can we find such a one as this is, a man in whom the Spirit of God is?
>
> Genesis 41:38

See what happened:

> And Pharaoh said unto Joseph, See, I have set thee over all the land of Egypt.

> And Pharaoh took off his ring from his hand, and put it upon Joseph's hand, and arrayed him in vestures of fine linen, and put a gold chain about his neck.

> And he made him to ride in the second chariot which

he had; and they cried before him, Bow the knee: and he made him ruler over all the land of Egypt.

And Pharaoh said unto Joseph, I am Pharaoh, and without thee shall no man lift up his hand or foot in all the land of Egypt.

Genesis 41:41-44

Friends, when God's eyes find you, they will put you where He wants you to be.

Righteousness is the shortest way to the topmost top. Stop that sin now, so it doesn't stop you tomorrow!

# BEAUTY

Purity gives birth to beauty.

Let's look again at that Tommy Hicks' prophecy:

*Slowly, this great giant began to rise and as he did, his head and hands went into the clouds. As he rose to his feet he seemed to have cleansed himself from the debris and filth that was upon him, and he began to raise his hands into the heavens as though praising the Lord; and as he raised his hands, they went even unto the clouds.*

*Suddenly, every cloud became silver, the most beautiful silver I have ever known.*

Friends, nothing glorifies, nothing beautifies like holiness!

It says, "*The cloud became silver...*" When the Church

will rise in holiness, rise in righteousness, there shall be beauty, heaven–decked beauty upon Zion! When men will come forth with a covenant oath — "If I perish, I perish! I will live for the truth!"

Having cleansed itself from the debris, that giant emerged in beauty — the cloud over her head became silver. *"The most beautiful silver I've ever seen"*, said Tommy Hicks. Oh yes! Purity gave birth to beauty!

Purity is the mother of beauty. Psalm 149:4 says, *"He will beautify the meek with salvation."* And what is salvation?

Talking about Jesus, Matthew 1:21 says, *"He shall save his people from their sins."*

So when you are saved from sin, your beauty emerges, your true colour, your covenant colour emerges. Your authority, your dominion is established.

We will go for purity, because it will surely deliver our beauty to us. When sin goes, beauty emerges.

I see your beauty emerge in a most powerful way!

I'd like you to know also that God's faithfulness is stronger than any attack that the quest for righteousness may bring your way.

## REJOICE AT PERSECUTIONS

Yea, and all that will live godly in Christ Jesus shall suffer persecution.

2 Timothy 3:12

By the inspiration of the Holy Spirit, I defined persecution as, "a display of emotional displeasure, which leads to unjust treatment. Borne out of hatred, bitterness, envy, misgivings, etc; it is the heritage of the frontliners".

Naturally, the seed of the bond woman is on a commission to persecute the child of promise. So when you are persecuted for righteousness sake, God is giving you a signal of lifting from heaven. God told me something on 1st March, 1992. He said:

*Hundredfold (of every blessing) will come with hundredfold of persecutions!*

*If you don't want to be persecuted, then you don't want to be blessed.*

*If you don't want to be backbitten, then get behind!*

*If you don't want to be pulled down, then choose to be on the ground.*

*If you don't want to be gathered against, then stay where they are.*

*In a race, only those behind see how the ones in front are running.*

*Man is a free moral agent, he must be allowed to speak what he sees.*

*If you don't want to be talked against, then you must quit the front.*

*You must allow all those who are behind you to do their job — see your back and talk at your back.*

You are beginning on a journey of holiness now, plenty of mockeries will come from wayfaring Christians, the ones who are not going anywhere. They are wayfaring, they just stand on the way. They are by the wayside, they are the seeds by the way side. The birds will soon come and pick them up.

You must allow those who are behind you to do their job: to see your back and talk at your back; to see your back and bite it.

Therefore, everyone who wants the blessings unconsciously wants the persecutions as well—that is, the lies, the mockeries, the slanders, the castigations, etc. If you don't know that these things are there, you will be tired!

Jesus said:

> Woe unto you, when all men shall speak well of you!
>
> Luke 6:26

## *Persecutions Bring Promotion*

Those who mind men naturally miss God. If I had minded men, I would have missed God long ago. You will not miss God!

So the Lord spoke to me, *"Develop yourself to enjoy persecutions. Just make sure you're not in error"*.

Persecutions are no afflictions, they are signals and proofs of promotion.

A brother heard the word that, "You must not give or take bribe". For 10 months, he was humiliated because he refused to give bribe. His friends perhaps mocked him. He was asked to return the one million naira cheque they gave him. Because they now knew his stand, they were out (as the children of the bond woman) to persecute him. But when they persecute you for your righteousness, it provokes God for your promotions.

When they persecuted Joseph for purity, God found a place for him in the palace! Every persecution for righteousness equals exaltation from heaven!

> Wherefore come out from among them, and be ye separate saith the Lord...then I will be your God and you will be my son.
>
> 2 Corinthians 6:17-18

This is your great hour for personal attention. Every child that runs from exams will remain in the same class. If you like, take sick leave when exams are around; that's not a certificate that you have passed. When you are well, you will still come back to do the exam. Everybody must write this exam we are talking about, or you won't go forward.

God said, *"Develop yourself to enjoy persecutions. They are no afflictions, they are signals of your promotion. God is out to stir up jealousy through you!"*

Every persecution against your righteousness is announcing your promotion.

## *Persecution Does Not Kill*

Rejoice at persecutions.

Note that persecutions are not just from sinners, but also from saints, preachers, and even your very close acquaintances.

You are going to write the tests of persecution, but you will pass them and you will see your promotions.

Please, expect persecutions! Develop yourself to enjoy them. Rejoice at them, because they are announcing your promotion.

Persecution does not kill, it is ignorance that kills.

Every greatness from heaven is welcomed on earth by persecutions.

When Moses was born, he was born into the midst of persecutions. Pharaoh had already announced that all male children should be killed.

When Jesus arrived (the Moses of the New Testament), persecution was waiting. Herod said, "Kill all the children born, because I have heard that a king is born". Hell has heard of your status now, and is setting traps to trap you. He will not catch you!

The persecutions of life are a reality. But your power over them is also a reality. So let your eyes be single.

What is the sole aim of persecutions? To stop the persecuted from attaining his goal. You will attain your goal for holiness and righteousness!

Anybody can call you any name, that's his opinion. If they call you a thief, just make sure you are not stealing. If they say you are a liar, just make sure you are telling the truth. Among liars, the only one telling the truth is reckoned as a liar. So leave them with their opinion. The Judge of the whole earth is watching. Don't fight them, so you don't lose your righteousness. Don't be embittered against them, so you don't defile your holiness.

If Jesus was minding the comments of the Pharisees, He would never have arrived heaven. If He was going with the Saducees, He would have been sad till eternity. Leave the Pharisees, Saducees and the scribes where they are, you just stick your life to Jesus! Wish everybody well, you would have overcome persecutions as well.

The persecutors have a ministry, let them carry it out. You take heed to your own ministry, don't bother about other people's ministries. You know where you are going, so don't look back.

May the love that you have for Him keep you away from all the horrors of persecution.

Heaven is the home of overcomers. So only those who sailed through in the temptations of life will find their place in heaven. I perceive that on the gates of heaven, they will write "The City of Overcomers". Because when I read the book of Revelation, I kept seeing, *"He that overcometh"*, *"He that overcometh"*. So only he that overcometh gets there. Heaven is the overcomer's city, only overcomers get there!

Blessed is the man that endureth temptation...

James 1:12

When you endure persecution, you win a crown; a crown of life. You are not enduring sin, but persecution. It's time to go and endure it.

Friends, there's a crown you're hunting for. You will not miss it!

# 10

# Be Sober!
# BeVigilant!

In this chapter, I want to share with you some of the ways to maintain this great touch of holiness in your life.

## NO CONTACT, NO CONTRACT!

Contact is what establishes contract. When contact is monitored, contract becomes impossible.

1 Thessalonians 5:22 warns:

Abstain from all appearances of evil.

Contact is the surest access to get into the trap of immorality. Immorality is impossible without contact. You remember Proverbs 7:13?

So she caught him, and kissed him...

Samson wouldn't have gone down, but that contact was too strong. He was right on the laps of Delilah! Then she had opportunity to press him with her words. She caught him and finished him!

Clean up! Until you tidy up your environment you never become tidy. Clean up! Your environment needs cleaning. That staff of yours with whom you cannot be relaxed, send him/her away now!

Friends, many kingdoms have been ruined! This one that God is building by us this time around will not be ruined. That's why we have to be cautious. Peter said:

> Wherefore gird up the loins of your mind, be sober, and hope to the end for the grace that is to be brought unto you at the revelation of Jesus Christ;
>
> As obedient children, not fashioning yourselves according to the former lusts in your ignorance:
>
> But as he which hath called you is holy, so be ye holy in all manner of conversation.
>
> Because it is written, Be ye holy; for I am holy.
>
> 1 Peter 1:13-16

It is so obvious that we are the apple of God's eye, and therefore the envy of hell. We must brace up!

Never mind those women who keep coming for deliverance. They are not possessed. Just like Satan entered into Peter to use him to distract Jesus from His mission, people around you can be entered into any second. That did not get Peter possessed; he was only used.

Do you know why God is sounding this alarm? Satan is out to use too many people this year, to corrupt our liftings. That's why we have two many bad examples now. You just must be careful, so you are not added to the list.

> Lust not after her beauty in thine heart, neither let her take thee with her eyelids.
>
> Proverbs 6:25

They will hunt for the precious. That is their mission. They will hunt! They will be fully armed! They will come crying and weeping. They know that you and I are precious in the sight of God, so they will come hunting.

You must vow with your life not to be caught.

## THE MYSTERY OF RIGHT COMPANY

> Be not deceived: evil communications corrupt good manners.
>
> 1 Corinthians 15:33

If you want to live right, keep the right company! Relate with the right things!

Somebody once shared a testimony of how he used to watch a certain programme on T.V., and how that

**207**

programme eventually led to his backsliding. He lost his eternal life for at least two years, before he returned home.

Friends, it's right company for right living!

No matter how anointed you are, no matter how dedicated you are, no matter how much vows you have made, evil communication will corrupt good manners any day!

The company you keep determines the life you live.

The Corinthian Church was the most gifted Church. The Bible says they were not behind in any gift of the Holy Spirit. In fact, speaking in tongues became like their natural language. So much so that Paul had to introduce order to the way they spoke in tongues in their gatherings.

He told them:

> Though I speak with the tongues of men and of angels, and have not charity, I am become as sounding brass, or a tinkling cymbal.
>
> And though I have the gift of prophecy, and understand all mysteries, and all knowledge; and though I have all faith, so that I could remove mountains, and have not charity, I am nothing.
>
> And though I bestow all my goods to feed the poor, and though I give my body to be burned, and have not charity, it profiteth me nothing.

1 Corinthians 13:1-3

So it was a knowledgeable and giving Church. They had understanding of mysteries. But by evil communication they were corrupted. As gifted and as knowledgeable as they were, they were the most corrupt Church in the New Testament days. Any kind of sin you could imagine was there! In fact, they used to fight at the communion table!

It was the most charismatic of all the Churches, yet it was so corrupt! They had the gift of the Spirit of holiness, the Holy Spirit was heavy upon them. Yet, evil communication corrupted them.

Proverbs 13:20 warns us:

> He that walketh with wise men, shall be wise: but a companion of fools shall be destroyed.

That Church was so polluted that in 1 Corinthians 5:1, we see one of them snatch his father's wife! They were so polluted! Because when they gave their lives to Christ, they did not separate from evil company. They still hung on with the "Old Boys Associations", they held on to their "childhood friends", they held on to their "club memberships".

How do I know all these? Well, see what Paul told them in 2 Corinthians 6:14-17:

> Be ye not unequally yoked together with unbelievers: for what fellowship hath righteousness with unrighteousness? and what communion hath light with darkness?

And what concord hath Christ with Belial? or what part hath he that believeth with an infidel?

And what agreement hath the temple of God with idols? for ye are the temple of the living God; as God hath said, I will dwell in them, and walk in them; and I will be their God, and they shall be my people.

Wherefore come out from among them, and be ye separate, saith the Lord, and touch not the unclean thing; and I will receive you.

I can imagine some of them saying, "Christianity does not mean we should abandon our friends. How will they get to know Jesus? If we separate from them, how will they know the Lord?"

Well, I've got bad news for you! It's easier for them to separate you from God, than for you to bring them to God!

Listen to me, Christianity that has no demarcation will lead to destruction!

How can you sit together with a sinner and be swimming in his counsel?

Blessed is the man that walketh not in the counsel of the ungodly, nor standeth in the way of sinners, nor sitteth in the seat of the scornful.

But his delight is in the law of the Lord; and in his law doth he meditate day and night.

And he shall be like a tree planted by the rivers of

water, that bringeth forth his fruit in his season; his leaf also shall not wither; and whatsoever he doeth shall prosper.

The ungodly are not so: but are like the chaff which the wind driveth away,

Therefore the ungodly shall not stand in the judgment, nor sinners in the congregation of the righteous.

Psalm 1:1-5

I am therefore asking you now to make your choice. It is impossible to live the holy life by getting into an accord with unholy people. When you stay with a liar, you partake of his lying spirit. He will make you a false witness. You can't make friends with an adulterer and not fall into the same sin.

When we started the Christian race, there were some of our brethren in those days who said they were taking the revival to their former churches. Now, they themselves are in need of revival, because they have "died" there! What is the living doing among the dead?

Proverbs 21:16 says:

The man that wandereth out of the way of understanding shall remain in the congregation of the dead.

May God deliver you from the trap of unbelievers! God said:

211

*Come out from among them, and be ye separate...*

As anointed as Jesus was, He remained among believers all through His stay here on earth. He chose the 12, that they might be with Him. So He had a registered company of men that surrounded Him. His confidants were Christians. John the beloved, had the closest access to His heart.

To have an unbeliever as your confidant makes a fool of your Christianity. Some of you say, "We were classmates in school". Well, get ready, because you will surely end up as prison mates eventually! Because hell is the greatest prison there is—it's a bottomless pit!

Friendship is not by force, it is by choice. Please don't play with your life! You are solely responsible for what becomes of your tomorrow. God won't call for a witness when He is judging you. So accept full responsibility for your life.

Many homes have been broken by friends. Some husbands' friends have polluted their minds against their wives. On the other hand also, some wives have friends that load them with destructive insinuations and so–called advices.

Evil communication corrupts good manners. You go to an ungodly man and you begin to share your genuine needs. He can only give you ungodly counsel, that will end up separating you from God!

Beware of men! Beware of men! Take heed where you stand or sit, to hear what you're hearing, so you don't destroy your life. Don't walk into the prison of evil friendship with your eyes wide open. Even a mad man knows a prison gate when he sees one.

Have you ever seen a mad man walk to the gates of a prison and say, "Open! Lock me inside"? No!

How then can you call someone who is against everything you stand for a friend? You stand for righteousness, he stands for sin. You stand for God, he stands for the devil. You stand for God, he stands for gold. Yet you say you're friends!

Listen, do you want to be free from adultery? Then disconnect from your adulterous friends. If you don't, they will disconnect you from God! No matter how strong you are as a man, if you go for pornographic magazines, the spirit of adultery and whoredom will settle upon you and possess you!

It is normal. It is contact that leads to contract. If you don't monitor contact, it will develop into contract in your disfavour.

Friends, hear this again: evil communication corrupts good manners! So be careful.

There are certain friends and relationships you must stop today, or they will stop you. Before you know it, you're already swimming in lies and adultery with them.

I don't have permanent friends, I only have permanent interests. The moment we are not on the same frequency, I'm gone! It is iron that sharpens iron. If I want to be a boxer, I will go to a boxer to train me. If I want to be a champion, I'll go to a champion to train me.

Friendship with the world is enmity with God (James 4:4). A friend of the world cannot be a friend of God. So make your choice. I would rather be received by God and rejected by men, than be rejected by God and received of men.

Paul said:

> Wherefore we labour, that, whether present or absent, we may be accepted of him.
>
> 2 Corinthians 5:9

## *Beware Of Ungodly Brethren*

> But now I have written unto you not to keep company, if any man that is called a brother be a fornicator, or covetous, or an idolater, or a railer, or a drunkard, or an extortioner; with such a one no not to eat.
>
> 1 Corinthians 5:9

So God is saying, friendship with the ungodly, "No!" With Christians who live ungodly lives, "No!"

Why am I saying all this? Let's look at Hebrews 10:26-27:

> For if we sin wilfully after that we have received

214

the knowledge of the truth, there remaineth no more sacrifice for sins.

But a certain fearful looking for of judgment and fiery indignation, which shall devour the adversaries.

A young lady for instance, who is determined to be free and has claimed God's grace for freedom, and later goes back to meet the same man, to renew the old contract, has gone back to her vomit. You will not be that person!

There is profit in purity. Godliness is profitable unto all things (1 Tim. 4:18). You will not be a loser in the world.

Awake unto righteousness!

Your lifestyle is largely determined by the company you keep. You cannot be brighter than the company you keep.

Friends, God's Word is strong on the company you keep, the counsel you receive, the place you stand and the place you sit (Ps. 1:1). They all go to determine whether you remain godly or ungodly.

God is saying, if you want your tomorrow to be secured, mind the counsel you draw from, mind the places you stand, mind the people you sit with. That is, mind the company you keep or you destroy your destiny.

The association you keep either makes or breaks you — it never leaves you neutral. It's either building you or breaking you. It's either lifting you or letting you!

Many people's Christianity is not in place today because of the friends they're keeping.

> ...a companion of fools shall be destroyed.
>
> Proverbs 13:20

With great price I purchased my liberty to go for God. Everybody gave up on me, for God to take me up. Won't you let God take you? Until He takes you, you're not secure.

If you don't break off from those unholy associations, they will bring you back to your vomit. But God forbid! Galatians 5:1 says:

> Stand fast therefore in the liberty wherewith Christ hath made us free, and be not entangled again with the yoke of bondage.

Having been fired up by God for a life of purity and holiness, this caution is important to maintain it. To maintain the flow of this holy fire, you need to mind the friends you keep. It is right company for right living!

There's no friend of a liar who can be free from lying. No way! You're either consenting to his lies by nodding your head or keeping quiet.

You need the right association, to enjoy the right manifestation. In any relationship, you're either growing or groaning, you're either being blessed or coming under a curse, you're either going up or coming down!

God has brought you this far, out of the miry clay, you will not return to your vomit!

The association you keep will either raise or erase you. It will either establish you or cause you to fumble. We have been raised up and made to sit together with Christ, so we are up. The ones who are not saved are down (on the ground). When you join them in friendship, you're walking on the edge of the cliff. You should be careful, because the nearer you are to the edge, the more dangerous it is!

A fifty–fifty Christian journey always ends in a crash! I have made up my mind to stay in the centre of the Kingdom, because one can fall headlong into hell from the edge of the cliff!

Watch out friend! You're too close to the edge! It's not safe!

Evil companionship will keep you in sin. Don't let your anointing or spiritual maturity deceive you, evil communication corrupts good manners. The scriptures cannot be broken!

Anyone that won't let you get to where you're going, separate from him or her! Those friends you had before you gave your life to Christ, leave them now, or they will drag you back to your vomit!

Evil association is an unclean thing. And God says, *"Touch not the unclean thing"*. When your best friend is an ungodly man, friends, you are in the "best" trap!

Hear this, if you still have a sinner as your best

friend after this kind of heavy visitation from heaven, you're looking for trouble! It's better to walk alone with God, than to be trapped with someone who scorns the truth, someone who defiles and mocks Jesus. You need friends who walk with God. You need associations that believe in your God, otherwise you will be trapped.

How can you have a company, a business, and make a sinner the Chairman or director? You don't need that kind of thing!

Sinners won't take you to any place of honour. They don't have it, they can't give it!

Go and remove that chairman! He is the reason you are going round on the same spot. Remove that uncle who is taking your company's name to the medicine man. If the devil catches you, he will torture you! If they won't go, leave the company for them and go start another one.

Let him that has ears hear what the Spirit is saying to the Church! If you have put yourself in chains, go and release yourself now! Don't wait till tomorrow.

You will not lose your place in God!

Wrong association is ungodly. It brings about all forms of ungodliness. Sin will continue as long as you keep wrong company.

There are people you visit and they drain you spiritually. You must stop it now, or they will stop you.

Why must you celebrate your relationship with a

liar, when you have made a choice for the truth? Why must you be visiting an adulterer, when you have made a choice for purity?

Break those relationships now before they break you!

## *The Jonadab Trap*

There was a young man called Amnon in 2 Samuel 13. He was one of the sons of David. He had a step brother called Absalom whose younger sister was called Tamar.

Amnon so desired his step sister Tamar, that he kept looking for a way to sleep with her. His lust made him so sick that he was losing weight. Then his friend Jonadab came on the scene. The Bible says;

> But Amnon had a friend, whose name was Jonadab, the son of Shimeah, David's brother.
>
> 2 Samuel 13:3

He asked Amnon:

> Why art thou, being the king's son, lean from day to day? wilt thou not tell me?
>
> verse 4

And Amnon told him:

> I love Tamar, my brother Absalom's sister.

So Jonadab organised a plan, an evil plan for him:

> And Jonadab said unto him, Lay thee down on thy bed, and make thyself sick: and whey thy father

cometh to see thee, say unto him, I pray thee, let my sister Tamar come, and give me meat, and dress the meat in my sight, that I may see it, and eat it at her hand.

verse 5

Note that Amnon was a covenant child, he had covenant blood in him. His father was God's choice on the earth. He had a connection with the covenant of purity. So he couldn't organise sin successfully. But he was cast down, trapped by the craftiness of a subtle friend—Jonadab.

See what happened:

And when she had brought them unto him to eat, he took hold of her, and said unto her, Come lie with me, my sister.

And she answered him, Nay my brother, do no force me, for no such thing ought to be done in Israel; do not thou this folly.

Howbeit he would not hearken unto her voice: but, being stronger than she, forced her, and lay with her.

verses 11-12,14

And at the end of it all, Absalom killed Amnon! (verses 28-29). And the same Jonadab went to David to announce the death of Amnon. May your friend not kill you and then go to announce your death.

Let every husband help his wife in her choice of

friends and let every wife also help her husband in his choice of friends.

It is right company, for right living! If your Christianity is still one-leg-in-one-leg-out, you don't have a future. If you don't have a friend you're relating with spiritually, you're already on your way to hell! Look for one now! Friendship is not by force, it's by choice.

God has been crying against adultery, fornication, stealing, lying, covetousness, idolatory. If you still go and make friends with the unrighteous mammon, you will mourn! Don't do it!

Do you want to be free from sin? Then look for godly saints as friends.

If you kill yourself, nobody will jump into the grave with you! No! Others will still be living. So think straight! Put on the armour of light!

> He that walketh with wise men shall be wise...
>
> Proverbs 13:20

I want you to go ahead and disengage every Jonadab in your boat. He's an agent of the devil to bring others down. Before he kills you, destroy that relationship! Would you?

There are places you must not enter anymore. There are things you must not share with anybody anymore. There are people that you must not take counsel from anymore.

There's no fifty–fifty in this thing. If you don't come out you'll cave in!

Since your Christianity has not been able to influence that your friend all these years, if you don't break away now, he will influence you to hell!

Your destiny is precious, the devil is looking for how to destroy it, but he will not succeed. You won't let him, will you?

Go and protect yourself.

> But he that is begotten of God keepeth himself, and that wicked one toucheth him not.
>
> 1 John 5:18

There is a great tomorrow for you.

Take your time to read the books of Corinthians and Romans. You will see how much you need to be careful in making friends, both with outsiders and insiders (unbelievers and believers). Make your choice, and let your choice be in line with what you stand for, and you will increase steadily in your righteousness.

## LET GO OF THOSE IDOLS!

> Little children, keep yourselves from idols.
>
> 1 John 5:21

In every major revival like this, quite a number are coming over from "Egypt" i.e, they just got born again. So they still have things under the bed, in the wardrobe. Things "my mother gave me", things "my father gave me".

And God spake all these words, saying,

I am the Lord thy God, which have brought thee out of the land of Egypt, out of the house of bondage.

Thou shalt have no other gods before me.

Thou shalt not make unto thee any graven image, or any likeness of any thing that is in heaven above, or that is in the earth beneath, or that is in the water under the earth.

Thou shalt not bow down thyself to them, nor serve them: for I the Lord thy God am a jealous God, visiting the iniquity of the fathers upon the children unto the third and fourth generation of them that hate me;

And shewing mercy unto thousands of them that love me, and keep my commandments.

Exodus 20:1-6

You become an enemy of God when you have any other thing you're leaning on besides Him. And it's a fearful thing to fall into the hands of the living God!

The Bible says that the sorrow of them that follow other gods shall be many. This could be why your sorrows have kept multiplying! Because you've been secretly following other gods somewhere, that only you know of.

Listen to this: God wants to put you on course this very hour. He wants to deliver you from the curses of life. Please, let Him do it!

Idolatory puts God off. It's a pollution in the sight of God. I want you to come out of every chain that the enemy has put around your feet.

If God be for you, who can be against you? (Rom. 8:31).

Idolatory puts God off!

You can't serve two masters, you must choose one and despise the other.

There are Christians who still have tiny, tiny things hidden in hideous corners in their homes, their offices, their cars, etc. Things they resort to time and time again. Some even still read the stars (horoscope) in the newspapers! All manner of pollutions! No wonder their sorrows are multiplying!

I don't care who gave that thing to you, I don't care where you found it, I don't care either for how long you've had it, if you don't let it go now, that's your end! Because there's a strong wind blowing. You either move with it or you're floored by it!

## *Even Human Idols!*

Graven images, human idols, they're all idols! These are the little godfathers and godmothers you've been leaning on. That's why the God of heaven left you alone.

There are people you worship to get one thing or the other from. That's why you're on the floor!

...If therefore thine eye be single, thy whole body shall be full of light.

Matthew 6:22

When you look away from God, you enter into darkness!

The cheapest way out of idolatory is to give God your total focus. God is more than enough!

Those godfathers and godmothers are the reason you're on the floor. Those graven images are the reason you're in the grave! It's time to come out! Idolatory is pollution in the sight of God.

In 1 Kings chapter 15, we see Asa returning to the Lord, but first he had to deal with his mother's gods.

And also Maachah his mother, even her he re-moved from being queen, because she had made an idol in a grove; and Asa destroyed her idol, and burnt it by the brook kidron.

1 Kings 15:13

He burnt it!

God wants every idol in your life burnt, otherwise you will get burnt!

It's fire! Whosoever keeps fire in his bossom and in his clothes will be burnt. That thing you're hiding some-where is the reason fire is burning in your life. Bring it out to be burnt, and your life will take a new shape.

Let's look at a story in Acts 19:11-14:

And God wrought special miracles by the hands of Paul:

So that from his body were brought unto the sick handkerchiefs or aprons, and the diseases departed from them, and the evil spirits went out of them.

Then certain of the vagabond Jews, exorcists, took upon them to call over them which had evil spirits the name of the Lord Jesus, saying, We adjure you by Jesus whom Paul preacheth.

And there were seven sons of one Sceva, a Jew, and chief of the priests, which did so.

These sons of the chief priests were exorcists! Sons of the chief priests! They were given to the devil. They were agents of the devil. Yet they were sons of the chief priest!

The high priest was their "Father", but they were given to idols. They were working with the devil!

See what happened to them! The Bible called them vagabonds! That is bastards, outcasts!

When a son of God begins to go about with the devil, he's seen as a vagabond. He becomes an outcast in the kingdom of God.

I don't know where you go after church, I don't know what you put on your lips before you come out in the morning, I don't know what is under your carpet in your office, I don't know what your mother gave you 15 years ago and which you still have since you gave your life to Christ! I don't know what you inherited from your father that you cherish so much that when your wife is coming, you're hiding it! But all things lay bare before Him. He sees all things, and God who sees you in secret begins to reward you openly!

To go after idols is to be a vagabond. Those young men were sons of the high priest, but they were vagabonds! And Satan tortured them!

You will not be tortured! But you will have to clean up!

In the midst of special miracles, in the midst of heavy movement of the Holy Spirit, some sons of the high priest were exorcists! They were native doctors! They were idol worshippers! It's like that with many sons of God. That's why their sorrows are multiplying! They pray, heaven is closed! They fast, God will not hear! Because there is something somewhere they are hiding from people, but God is seeing it!

And the evil spirit answered and said, Jesus I know, and Paul I know; but who are ye?

And the man in whom the evil spirit was leaped on them, and overcame them, and prevailed against them, so that they fled out of that house naked and wounded.

And this was known to all the Jews and Greeks also dwelling at Ephesus; and fear fell on them all, and the name of the Lord Jesus was magnified.

And many that believed came, and confessed, and shewed their deeds.

Many of them also which used curious arts brought their books together, and burned them before all men: and they counted the price of them, and found it fifty thousand pieces of silver.

So mightily grew the word of God and prevailed.

verses 15-20

You must not allow yourself to become a specimen of destruction in these mighty, great manifestations of the church.

Any other thing you bow to will burn you!

See what happened to them—they were wounded and stripped naked, because they had something in hiding that they did obeisance to. You will not be wounded! You will not be naked!

And many that believed came, and confessed, and shewed their deeds.

**verse 18**

They exposed their evil deeds, they brought their graven images out! They confessed and brought their idols.

Many of them also which used curious arts brought their books together, and burned them before all men; and they counted the price of them, and found it fifty thousand pieces of silver.

verse 19

All manner of charms made for you by your fathers, all the things that your parents sent to you from the village, it's time to bring them out to be burnt!

If you don't bring them out to be burnt, they will soon burn you before all men. There's a baptism of holiness going on now. This is your chance to be free, if it's your desire!

Those hidden things and idols are what are afflicting your family, afflicting your business, afflicting your children! When God is against you, everything is against you!

This revival is not just for any kind of person, it's for people who are ready! If you won't let go your idols, leave God alone! God does not need you, He is not looking for you! Your money is stinking in His sight, carry your money, go to hell, to your father the devil!

I know whom I have believed and I can see His mighty hand rest on His Church!

God doesn't need your money. Your position is worthless! It is your status in redemption that matters to heaven! You have a chance now to be free, if you want to! You can't be a vagabond in the Father's house!

You better take your place in God now, or you'll be cast out to the outer darkness, where there's weeping and gnashing of teeth (Matt. 25:30).

You can't serve two masters! If you are ashamed of God, He will be ashamed of you!

This God that I serve, He treats me well! I have been with Him for 28 years now. He's sweeter everyday.

This is the gospel of the New Testament order: *"they confessed and brought them forth..."*

Then:

> So mightily grew the word of God and prevailed.
>
> verse 20

That means, those things were resisting the Word; but when they were burnt, the Word of God grew mightily and prevailed. That idol is the reason the Word of God is not growing in your heart!

All those federal ministers that you are leaning on is the reason your business is down! All those government idols in your life are the reason you're on the ground!

His name is El-shaddai! He's more than enough!

At the end of this cleaning that we are in now, so mightily will grow the Word of God and prevail in your life! When you open your mouth, the devil will be shivering, because he has no part in you!

Jesus said:

> The prince of this world cometh, and hath nothing in me.
>
> John 14:30

Satan will not have any part in you anymore!

If you have any other god, you are a misfit in the Kingdom.

Some people say, "Since I gave my life to Christ, things have just been going downwards..." It is because of that thing in your life that you've not taken care of.

I met Jesus in 1969, and my life has not gone backwards once since then! No! I have never had a better last year in my life!

Any other thing you add to God makes Him leave you. But from now on, I see God settle with you in person!

Stop looking at somebody else, look at yourself now! What is that idol? Human idol? Position idol? Graven image? Look at it and tell yourself, "Enough is enough! I am going on with Jesus!"

James was speaking in Acts 15:19-20:

> Wherefore my sentence is, that we trouble not them, which from among the Gentiles are turned to God:

> But that we write unto them, that they abstain from pollutions of idols, and from fornication, and from things strangled, and from blood.

So if you have left fornication and you have not left idols, you have not left anything. If you have left adultery, but not idolatory, you have not left anything at all!

The Bible says:

> A double minded person is unstable in all his ways.

> For let not that person think that he shall receive any thing of the Lord!
>
> James 1:8,7

So, such a person will remain on the other side of

lack and want! He will pray and God will not hear, because he's double-minded. His mind is on that thing under his pillow or that one inside his pocket.

I have seen many vehicles that had charms hanging in front and still had accidents. Where were the charms when the cars had accidents? The charms could not help them. It was the charm that brought the jam!

But this Jesus that I serve, I have passed through death 19 times without a scratch! *Many are the afflictions of the righteous, but the Lord delivereth him out of them all. He keepeth his bones, and not one of them is broken!* (Ps. 34:19-20). The righteous is protected by heaven! When you camp with God, you camp with good! From this day, evil will not come near your house anymore, in the name of Jesus!

That cloudy place you go to that your friend does not know about, the neighbour you live with does not know your movement at all; but they see some people coming to your house, they see you kneeling down for them to put things on your head, it's enough now! You cannot serve two masters!

> Know ye not that the unrighteous shall not inherit the kingdom of God? Be not deceived; neither fornicators, nor idolaters, nor adulterers, nor effeminate, nor abusers of themselves with mankind,
>
> Nor thieves, nor covetous, nor drunkards, nor revilers, nor extortioners, shall inherit the kingdom of God.

And such were some of you: but ye are washed, but ye are sanctified, but ye are justified in the name of the Lord Jesus, and by the Spirit of our God.

1 Corinthians 6:9-11

*"But such were some of you"*. "Were", not "are"; so idolatory must be past tense in you life.

Let God be true and all men be liars.

If you love your father or mother or uncle more than Him, you are not worthy of Him. I love Jesus, He's all I want. Nothing matters to me near how much Jesus matters to me in this world. I will follow you only to the extent that you don't derail me from Christ.

It's over to you now! Whatever has been burning you before, God will burn it this time around.

And ye became followers of us, and of the Lord, having received the word in much affliction, with joy of the Holy Ghost.

So that ye were ensamples to all that believe in Macedonia and Achaia.

For from you sounded out the word of the Lord not only in Macedonia and Achaia, but also in every place your faith to God-ward is spread abroad; so that we need not to speak any thing.

For they themselves shew of us what manner of entering in we had unto you, and how ye turned to God from idols to serve the living and true God.

1 Thessalonians 1:6-9

**233**

I'd like you to know this: your will is strong enough to get the job done.

Have you ever seen a handsome or prosperous herbalist in your life? That's why I say idols make life dull! But look at the Jesus people all around!

Maybe you've kept that thing in ignorance, saying, "Well, I have given my life to Christ, it doesn't matter anymore..." It matters you know! You didn't know, but it matters!

There's a young man called Manasseh, he became a king at the age of 12. He led Israel into idolatory, sorceries, witchcraft, wizardry, he even built altars for idols in the house of God! Ah! Manasseh was a terrible man! But God afflicted him (2 Kgs. 21:1-18).

Idolatory brings affliction! That's why all native doctors look like guinea worms! They look like people who have no breath in them. I have never seen an attractive herbalist in this world! But come and see Jesus people! Blossoming, flourishing, refreshed, peaceful, established. That's where you are!

Why are you following the blind, when you can see?

Oh! Your father loves you, but he's blind. Will you let him direct the traffic while you're driving? When he says, "Turn to the left", you say, "Since he's my father, I will turn". And on the left is a gutter!

All those idol-fathers and idol–mothers are the reason your life is dull! Drop them now, and face God!

# 11

# It's Time To Clean Up!

Whoso despiseth the word shall be destroyed: but he that feareth the commandment shall be rewarded.

Proverbs 13:13

Friends, I'd like you to be sensitive in the spirit. If you've not started taking steps in the direction of the things you've encountered in this book so far, you are already in delusion.

These things are not for another man, they're for you, because it is your hour of visitation.

Balaam said, "Lord, shall I go on?" (You remember Balak was offering him some gain to curse the children of Israel.) God did everything to stop him, but because he wasn't ready to stop, he was destroyed! An angel stood on the way to stop him, still he was asking, "Lord, shall I go on?" So the Lord said," Go!" (Num. 22:35).

Before you are abandoned, decide on your return home. God abandoned Balaam to his destruction. You will not be abandoned!

This is a divine visitation going on now, you mustn't miss it!

Clean up! Time is running out!! Clean up! Fire is about to descend on the mountain!

Wash your clothes! The mountain will soon begin to smoke with His presence!

Clean up! Time is running out! This message is not for your neighbour, it is sent to you. Because the sounding of the trumpet is to prepare men for battle (1 Cor. 14:8).

Whatever you've heard in the past is fun, from now on, it's battle! And it is in battles you have casualties. It is now battle! So watch it, to be sure you don't fall a victim.

It is now war!

Every time you hear God saying something intensely, destruction is at the door! Every blowing of the trumpet is to mobilise men for battle.

Please recognise that this is your hour of visitation. It must not be despised. If you escape a cleansing now, it means you are simply doomed for destruction!

Remember purity is the booster of power. You put new wine in new bottles. Until your bottle becomes new, you can't experience the new anointing.

It's time to slay sin, before it slays you. To continue in it is a danger, don't toy with it!

The former things God has overlooked, He now commands that you repent. Don't go back to what is gone. But what happens from now on counts in your record with God.

To miss heaven with your eyes wide open, and die on the laps of Delilah and Jezebel will make you the biggest fool of all ages! God forbid that after hearing all that you have heard, you should be a victim of such a calamity!

Remember I said many have crossed the ninth time, and are just about to hit "*these ten times*". This is why God is sounding this alarm today. You love Him, yes! But prove it by pleasing Him. You can go any length for Him, yes! But it's time to prove it by pleasing Him.

The beauty of salvation is in righteousness. Let's go back and fasten our seat belts, and be determined under God, for a stainless Christian walk. And God is going to match it with stainless glory from heaven, upon everything that has to do with you.

Certain relationships must go! Certain connections must be dropped. If you don't drop them now, they will drop you tomorrow.

Sin is a reproach to any people. You may not see the reproach the first or second day or even the third day. But surely, it's coming! If you don't stop that sin, someday it will come face to face to stop you.

I'd like you to be determined today for righteousness.

God is saying:

... I have set before you life and death, blessing and
cursing: therefore choose life, that both thou and
thy seed may live.

Deuteronomy 30:19

Stand on your feet (like that giant)! The debris must
give way! The filthy garment must go! Walk into
your liberty! Isaiah 60:1 says:

Arise, shine; for thy light is come, and the glory of
the Lord is risen upon thee.

We are talking about total redemption in Christ. Sin
was the beginning of shame for man, righteousness
is the only way to have honour restored.

"*You have not seen glory yet,*" saith the Lord. "*I am only
preparing you for realms of glory you have never seen.*

*If you will clean up, and be holy as I am holy, I will visit
you with My beauty. Your purity will provoke the release
of My power.*

*The world will seek My knowledge from you. You are
going to see Me in a way you have never seen Me before.*

*I am cleaning you up to manifest you to the world.*

*I am preparing you to declare your sonship.*

*I am making you ready to occupy your throne*", saith
the Lord God of Hosts.

When sins are forgiven, refreshing and healings
follow (1 John 1:9). Miracles are released when sins

238

are forgiven. After God has forgiven your sins, access to every other thing becomes automatic.

The seed of all evils is sin. Now that you have repented, and the seed is no more in you, you can't have its fruits anymore.

The seed of Satan is sin. And his fruits are diverse things—fornication, adultery, stealing, lying, and so on. Now, because the seed is not there, the fruits have no right to manifest. Sickness, barrenness, failure, depression, frustration, and so on are all fruits of sin. Now sin has gone, they all must leave you alone. They must go!

> Wherefore, beloved, seeing that ye look for such things, be diligent that ye may be so found of him in peace, without spot, and blameless.
>
> 2 Peter 3:14

And Romans 13:14 adds:

> But put ye on the Lord Jesus Christ, and make not provision for the flesh, to fulfil the lusts thereof.

Please, arise and take your stand in God now! The night is far spent, the day is at hand!

I'd like you to know this: we are in the season of sanctification in the body of Christ. This sanctification will bring you your long–awaited restoration, and that restoration will release you into your realm of manifestation. You will not only be free, you will become an instrument of freedom among men!

It's time to arise! The world is waiting for you. When you sound in your room, your voice will be heard across the seas! When you speak on the phone, cancer will dissolve in a far–away country!

The world is waiting to hear you, don't let the devil destroy you!

Clean up! Clean up!! Clean up!!! He that will come is at the door!

This is my prayer for you:

- ⊃ Sin shall no longer have dominion over your life!

- ⊃ Your choice will stand in every conflict with sin!

- ⊃ Your choice for holiness today will remain a testimony in your life many years to come.

- ⊃ All that see you shall know that you are called by the name of the Lord, and they shall be afraid of you,

in Jesus precious name!

Peace!

# 12

# We Have Proofs!

Look at these testimonies:

"*Dear Bishop,*

*I use this wonderful opportunity to testify that God is truly a living God and that you are a true prophet of God.*

*I am into the business of promotions and events management. I handle promotions for many companies; but each time I do any business with this company which happens to be my major client, the guys who are responsible for the jobs ask for so much in return as kick–backs. I had been servicing them and each time I settle them I get broke and my company is in trouble, to the point that we run helter-skelter to pay salaries. To feed even becomes a big problem.*

*In January, 1996, you instructed that we should not give bribe to any one, and I had just finished a major promotion for this same company, and the guys were expecting me to bring their returns. I became confused as to what to do, but I eventually obeyed your instruction and did not give the guys anything.*

241

*Then trouble started! They started to black–mail me and refused to give me any more jobs. People told me to go and beg them, but I refused, because I was acting on your instructions. Things became rough, but I held on to the instruction.*

*I then decided to start talking to some other compa-nies, for them to show interest in our major event of the year that holds in December. I found another company in June and after several meetings, they agreed they were going to sponsor the event on the condition that the first company be part of it, because they did not want to be seen as stealing an event that another company had been involved with for some years back.*

*So, they requested for a meeting with the first company and told them their mind and the first company agreed to all their request. But unknown to me and the other company, they had their own plans. Arrangements began and all hands were put on deck for us to have two multi-national companies sponsoring this event and it was going to be a bang. On October 24th, 1996, I received a cheque of one million naira from the second company, as their own share for sponsorship of the event. I was expecting to collect another one million naira from the first company as their own share too.*

*On 28th of October, 1996, I paid in the one million naira cheque into the bank and went to the office to do some paper work. And as I finished praying, my secretary told me that I had a visitor and I said the person should come in. The person I saw was the brand manager of the brand*

and company that gave me the one million naira cheque. She said the first company had pulled out of the deal, so I should not pay the cheque into my account, and that her company might not continue the deal since the agreement we had was that the two companies must do the event.

I did everything I could, but they had made up their minds not to go ahead, since the first company had pulled out. I later found out that the guys deliberately led us on to enable them disappoint us, because I refused to give them their usual bribe in January.

Somehow, I refused to lose hope, as I remembered and held on to your testimony of having lost your bag at the airport sometime ago and how you did not worry. My wife and I came to church, but I could not wait, so my wife met with a pastor and they both prayed together.

On Tuesday, I received a letter requesting that I return the cheque. So on Tuesday, 29th October 1996, I returned the one million naira cheque and I said one prayer — 'God, if it is You that sent Bishop Oyedepo to say we should not give bribe and I listened to him and this happened, over to You'. I returned the cheque without any ill feelings. My staff were all upset and I told them not to worry, saying, 'God is in control'.

When I got back from returning the cheque, I met another letter from some people requesting for a meeting with me. Apparently, they had been looking for me for a while. Somebody who had seen one of my events got to South Africa and mentioned it to them, and they wanted to set up an office in West Africa, with headquarters in Nigeria.

*I went for the meeting and what did I come out with? They wanted me to be their head in West Africa, moving my office to Ikoyi from Ikeja, all expenses paid by them! Presently, they have bought me a brand new car valued at 2.2 million naira! I arrived Nairobi today (all expenses paid) on course, and for Christ sake, what I got is unbelievable! First class treatment, five star hotel etc!*

*I decided to write to you, to personally say, 'Bishop, THANK YOU'; for your words, for everything. Words are not enough to describe my appreciation. I also want to specially thank God for everything. The package I have is extremely unbelievable! I thank God. Bishop, I love you with the whole of my heart."*
— *Onime, K.*

## He Gave Up That Business

"I'm a Nigerian, but I live in Banjul, The Gambia. I came to Nigeria on 19th December, 1996. I want to testify of what the Lord has done in my life since I met the World Mission Agency in Banjul, The Gambia.

I am a businessman, who used to deal in illegal business. But the day I came in contact with the World Mission Agency, I decided to give up that business, because I received the Word of life from them. I stood upon this Word of life and the day I gave up that business, God just transformed my life!

I came to Nigeria, to minister to my parents, who had not received Christ before. And glory be to God, they received Christ the very day I returned. I thank God for what He is doing in the lives of the people in Gambia through the WMA missionaries. I'm amazed at what is going on there myself. I also want to thank the Bishop. Everyone is waiting for his visit to The Gambia."

— Okonkwo, C.

## *"God...I Want To Live A Holy Life"*

"I thank the Bishop and I thank God, for making him to send that word unto me yesterday. Since Sunday when that bomb (the message preached) came to me, things have turned around in my life.

I used to be a womanizer, a real one. But after hearing that sermon on Sunday, I couldn't get up from my seat to walk home. When I got home, the landlord asked me, 'What happened? Are you sick?' I said no. The Bishop said, 'If you have all those useless things of the world in your house, throw them away'. So on getting home, I gathered all the useless pictures I used to take in those days and tore them all.

When I desired to be close to God, I asked Him what I could do and I joined the sanctuary keepers. But despite this, the devil kept tempting me.

I am an automobile electrician. There is no way we would do any job without telling lies. We would always inflate the price of things bought. I then said, 'God, I need a change. I want to live a holy life'. And the word preached yesterday hit me again. The Bishop said, 'If you are in a place where evil is done, but you don't join them, you also partake in the curse that befalls them'.

**245**

When I came to clean the sanctuary this morning, I looked on the notice board and saw a vacancy advert for a driver. I have six years experience in driving, so, I copied the address and went in search of the place. It is a new nursery/primary school. I met a teacher there, who said the proprietress was not around. She confirmed that they actually needed drivers to drive the school bus and a personal driver for the proprietress.

I then decided to walk down to my former office, to say hello to them and then go home. On getting there, they still wanted me to continue working, but I told them, I didn't want to work with them again. While still saying hello to them, a relation drove in. He said they had been looking for me for many days. I told him I was no longer working here, that I was looking for another job, because I wanted to live a holy life.

He said, 'We have been looking for you. We want to buy a bus for you. In fact, I'm just coming from where I went to price the bus'. He said, the bus he priced was going for 410,000 naira! He said we would go to the place together tomorrow, so I can make my choice of bus!"
— Ezekiel, S.

## "I've Stopped My Crave And Love For Money!"

"Being ruled by the god of gold, I got involved in drug trafficking. I take drugs to the United States of America and at times bring it in from Thailand.

A cousin of mine who worships here had always invited

me to this church, but I refused. Instead, I go to another church, where I'm given something to use. After using whatever I'm given, I think I'm okay. But despite all these, I got into problem and I was arrested and detained.

I said, 'Money would do it'. I didn't know the Lord. My business partners came together and raised money to bribe my way out of the place. I believed so much in their bribes that I was convinced that I would be released. But I wasn't released!

The first year came and went, the second year rolled by. I was taken to prison. Then I knew that the end had come.

When I got there, I met people worshipping God. In fact, some people came to me, inviting me to God. But I rebuffed them. My cousin who worships here kept sending books to me and my younger brother also sends the anointing oil.

Then one day, something ministered to me, 'You will die here O! If you don't know God, you will die here'.

I'd never fasted in my life, but I then began to fast; I started doing dry fasting. I found myself able to fast and pray for three days at a stretch. People spent a lot of money to get me out of prison, but did not succeed and after some time they began to be weary. And when they got tired, I said, 'God will do it'.

Though all my needs in the prison were supplied (as people kept bringing money to me), I was desperate to be released. So on April 22nd, 1994, I accepted Christ into my life. I began to know God and to have faith in Him, that He would set me free. And miraculously, in February

*1996, a way opened for me. I was arraigned in court and instead of my being jailed at least 25 years (because of the quantity of substance found on me), I was jailed for 5 years. My sentence started reading from the day I was arrested, so I was set free immediately!*

*And since I was released from jail, God has been doing a wonderful thing in my life. I've never missed a service here. And whenever I come, the Bishop's preaching always touches me, especially his teachings during the Signs and Wonders Week. And now, I've stopped my crave and love for money. I've cut off from all my friends, who still come to convince me to continue in the drugs business. I'm free now, and the Lord has been supplying all my needs, according to His riches in glory."*

*— O.K.*

## *"I've Now Exalted Righteousness..."*

*"On Monday, as soon as I alighted from the bus that brought me to church, my heart began to beat so fast, I began to be afraid. That wasn't the first time that the spirit of fear would come upon me. A sister took me to the Healing Room. I thank God that the Lord delivered me from that affliction that day. I've not been afraid since then.*

*Since the Bishop began to preach about sin on Monday, I began to confess all that the Spirit of the Lord laid in my heart to confess. And I thank God that I've now exalted righteousness in my life.*

*When I had my baby on November 18th 1996, the milk*

*from my breast had not been flowing. But since this Signs and Wonders Week began, the milk has started flowing very well now! Also, since I had that baby, I was afflicted with internal heat. I feel something moving in me, from my head to my toe. But since yesterday, it all stopped."*
— Adebayo, V.

## Boils Burst, After Forgiveness

"When I heard of the Signs & Wonders Week, I was prepared for it. But when I came for the service on Monday, I was in heavy pains, with boils in about five places all over my body.

When the Bishop said it was only holiness that would bring us close to God, I prayed (because he asked us to pray for forgiveness), then I asked for healing. I went home in pains and could not come to church on Tuesday.

I anointed myself, particularly the spots of the boils. And by Wednesday morning, the boil burst and I'm now relieved, with all the pains gone!"
— Erhator, S.

## Spirit Of Immorality Destroyed

"For about 12 years, I was held captive by the spirit of immorality. I gave my life to Christ in 1994 and when I read Proverbs 7:13-14, I began to cry. But this Spirit still didn't go.

I then made up my mind to wait on the Lord in the Word during this Signs & Wonders Week. And I was healed totally from the spirit of immorality.

*Also, I suffered from pile since 1990. It first came as haemorroids. I took all sorts of drugs and native herb's. It subsided, but resurfaced last year and my anus was sticking out and I was drying up. But this week, I decided to wait on the Lord for my healing. And now, I'm totally healed!"*
— *Adepoju, O.*

## 15 Yrs Marijuana Addict Delivered!

"I started worshipping here in July 1996. I was a marijuana addict for about 15 years. I got addicted while in secondary school. I've tried to stop the addiction on several occasions, because my whole family was against it. In fact, this has hindered me from attaining my goals in life.

*But when I started worshipping here, I took the anointing oil after praying, and that was the end of the 15 years bondage! And since then, good things began to manifest in my life.*

*I was in the bank before, but was relieved of the job. I later set up my own company, an agro allied and food processing equipment company.*

*Since I started worshipping here, things have started flourishing for me. I've been getting jobs worth 200,000 and one million naira. Also, I was recently given a free-lance marketing post in a newspaper house, which can fetch me about 50,000 naira monthly."*
— *Sumonu, K.*

## *"I Made Up My Mind...To Live Righteously."*

*"I'm a footballer. We were in closed camp last year, while preparing for the challenge cup competition. I had an evil attack in the night, something held me down to the bed and I was being choked. When I got up, I started feeling terrible; I had internal heat, headache and several other symptoms. I couldn't tell what was wrong with me.*

*I had to go to the doctor, (my team officials took me to the doctor). And after several tests, they told me that I was alright, that there was nothing wrong with me. But the heat, headache and all, still persisted. At one of our away matches, I almost fainted in the stadium. I had to be stretched out. I then had to leave my club camp in mid season, and came down to Lagos. I reasoned within myself that if I was to die, then I should die in Lagos, where my parents live.*

*In Lagos, I ran into a friend, who worships here. He administered the anointing oil to me in his house and I felt relieved a bit. That made me to believe for the first time. I then decided to start worshipping here. I started coming, and my condition started improving, though I still felt pains in my knees and legs. I was still unable to try out on road walks and my usual workouts.*

*Two days ago, the Bishop kept talking about righteousness, that if we wanted to be healed of all ailments in our bodies, then we should start living righteously. I thought within myself that I was probably not healed because I was still doing things that I knew was wrong. I then made up my mind to put all those things aside and to live righteously.*

**251**

I was here yesterday and on my way home, I discovered that I was relieved of the pains. This morning, I tried out on roadwalk. I did a 10 kilometre road walk and I discovered that all the pains were gone!"

— Chike, P.

## *"I Was A Master Fabricator Of Lies"*

"I used to indulge in everything you can think of a young boy indulging in, except smoking. And since I got born again last year, I started trying to stop all these things. I used to go out with a lot of girls. And I also indulged in lying. I took lying as impossible to stop. I thought one couldn't stop lying, even after being born again.

But at the January Signs and Wonders Week, the Bishop said, 'If you take holiness to be unachievable, you will die in sin'. I then prayed to God, that I wanted to stop lying. Before, I was a master fabricator of lies! Whenever my friends were in trouble, they would come to me and say, 'Dare, this is what we want, this is how it is'. After telling me everything, I would help fabricate a lie that would settle the matter.

After hearing the Bishop, however, I told God I wanted to stop lying. And glory be to God, yesterday, I was just thinking and I cast my mind back, trying to remember when last I lied. One of the pastors said the devil is like shit to us, that he has no value. That's how lying and every form of sin is to me now! I give God the glory."

— K. J.

## "*I Stopped Smoking Marijuana!*"

"I would say I was just like Saul (Paul the Apostle); I never for one day believed a Christian could walk into the church and stand to give a testimony.

My wife started coming here after we had a lot of problems because of where we were worshipping before. We used to belong to one of these sects and after a while, we had a problem. But she started coming here last year. And whenever she returns home after the service, I would beat her. The whole estate always gathered in my house any day she goes to church, because I would beat her.

They kept pleading with me not to beat her to death, but I promised that I would keep beating her as long as she kept coming here. She kept coming here and I kept beating her. On Christmas Eve, I sent her packing, to her relatives; but she still kept coming here from there. Her family came to try and reconcile us, but I insisted that she chose between me and the church. She still kept coming from the shop to church.

I then decided to come here, to see what her attraction here was; I was convinced that there was a man behind it all. I called some of my friends to accompany me here and we came in a vehicle that I had planned to use in packing out her things from my house to the church. If I met her with a man.

When we got to the gate, the crowd was too much and my friends said, 'Ah, we can't stay here. This place is too big for us,' and they ran away. Then I saw my wife and she said, 'Come inside, they won't hurt you'.

It took me time to decide to give my life to Christ,

*because I come from a Christian home (my father is a Methodist Reverend), and I have been around, in search of the right way of worshipping God. But after listening to the Bishop that day, I said to myself, 'This man is a vessel that God is using'. I found his teachings extraordinary, different from all the teachings I've heard before. I then decided to give my life to Christ, which I did on the 12th of January.*

*Unknown to my wife, I had been smoking Marijuana for the past 30 years. She lives in the same house with me, but each time she came into my room, I would tell her, 'Go away, I'm praying', and she would leave. But after I accepted Christ on the 12th (six days after my 40th birthday), I stopped smoking Marijuana! I've been vomiting the residue in my inside since then.*

*Also, I'd been using glasses for the past 15 years. But in the last week of January, the Bishop was praying and suddenly, I couldn't see again! But when I removed the glasses, I started seeing very well! I can now read my small print Bible!*

*I thank Jesus for all the good things He has done for me. Now, my neighbours no longer come to settle our fights; rather, laughter is what they hear from our home and the peace of the Lord has settled in my home!"*

— O. H.

# If You're Not SaveD, You're Not SafE!

## Look at this testimony:

"I was born and brought up as a Muslim and was initiated into a cult when I was young. And four years ago, I was afflicted and from then on, things began to get tough and rough for me. I went through hell. I went to all manner of native doctors in Lagos and 'alfas' did all sorts of sacrifices, killing rams and all sorts of animals, but all to no avail. This affliction almost resulted in mental affliction late last year. I get so angry that I feel like killing people. I kept to myself, without talking to anyone for days.

I gave my life to Christ, and since then, things began to change. Things are okay with me now! I no longer get angry and can now retain my money and spend it prudently, unlike before when it used to disappear mysteriously. I'm doing very fine!"
— I, E. E.

---

Have you ever asked Jesus to come into your heart? That is, are you BORN AGAIN?

If your answer is "NO", or you are not sure, please pray this prayer with all sincerity and confidence:

*Lord Jesus, I come to You today.*

*I am a sinner, I cannot help myself.*

*Forgive me my sins. Cleanse me with Your precious blood.*

*Deliver me from sin and Satan, to serve the Living God.*

*Today, Lord Jesus, I accept You as my Lord, and my Saviour.*

*Thank You Jesus, for saving me! Now I know, I am born again!*

**Book Encounters**

Dr. David Oyedepo's books are anointed spiritual weapons with which many have fought battles over sickness, poverty, failure, oppressions, etc, and won! It is so evident that the liberating anointing upon the words he speaks on the pulpit also rests upon the words in print. Diverse testimonies have been coming in to prove this.

## Hear these:

"For almost three years I had been trying to sell some caterpillar parts I brought from France but could not get buyers and they were becoming rusty. But as I was reading Dr. Oyedepo's book, Breaking Financial Hardship, I got to page 109, where the Bishop was talking about "Compromising Your Integrity" and I began to receive fast understanding of my problem in selling these parts. Not only this. I got to page 112, and he said, "Right dealings do not reduce men's height, it promotes and sustains it", referring to Luke 16:10-11. I could not go any further; immediately, I realised my past dirty dealings in business. I went on my knees and asked God to forgive me and vowed to avoid ungodly dealings in my business.

Few days later, I received a call from one of my friends, who told me that he had seen a man looking for caterpillar parts. I supplied these parts and even made double gain on it!

— Kouda, M.

"My ill health began over three years ago, though I began to experience the symptoms and signs a year later. They pointed to HIV/AIDS. As it persisted and progressed, I went for a full blood count examination, and the result still pointed to HIV, with marked W.B.C. count.

One day while praying, the Lord pointed to me His Word and said that was all I needed. He said all I needed was the truth that would set me free, but before that, I needed faith which comes by hearing and hearing by the Word of God. I surely had to settle down with two books written by Bishop David Oyedepo, Keys to Divine Health and Understanding Vision and several tapes. I took the holy communion, then the following day I went to the man in charge of AIDS counselling and told him that I wanted to have another lab examination. On 2nd January, 1997, I went to collect my results, and it was negative!

Also, when I went to do a full blood count it was very normal and I knew Jesus had restored my health. The devil brought pains all over, to look as though I had not received my healing, but as I continued to confess my healing, it disappeared and I have never experienced them again! Blessed be His name for ever."

— K, J. K.

*Following is a display of some titles by Dr. DAVID OYEDEPO* ▷

# BreakThrough TAPES!

## AUDIO & VIDEO

## *This Will Inspire You...*

After I received my Christmas bonus in January, I gave my pastor the whole package (minus my tithe) and asked him to buy all of the Bishop's books and as many tapes as the money I gave him can purchase. In March, I listened to one of those tapes. The Bishop said, "This is your peak and if you miss your peak, you'll end up in a pit. This is your time and you must take time to make that count." So, I sacrificed the month of April to come for the WOFBI Bible school course. I wasn't paid for that month. When I got back to the office after the course, there was a letter waiting for me, that I should report at the head office in Lagos, to go through the workers' evaluation sheet. And yesterday while in the office, I got a radio phone, which said, "Bro. Nath, what is happening? I discovered that we are owing you 300 tonnes of granite. What do you want us to do?" And my reply was, "Please dispose of them immediately and send me the money." And in less than three hours, my project manager bought 300,000 naira to me! He also went on to say, "I discovered we didn't pay you in April. I will pay you your salary from my pocket." And he did exactly that!

— A, N. B.

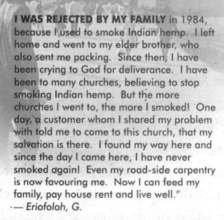

# The Author

For more than two decades, Dr. David O. Oyedepo, has been part of the current charismatic renaissance sweeping through the African continent. His faith-based teachings have transformed millions of lives.

Called with a specific mandate to liberate mankind from all oppressions of the devil.

Dr. Oyedepo is the Presiding Bishop of Living Faith Church Worldwide with a network of churches all over Nigeria and most nations of Africa.

He is the Senior Pastor of the 50,000 capacity - Faith Tabernacle, Canaanland, Ota, reputed to be the largest church auditorium in the world.

As an educationist, his mission currently pioneers the establishment of educational institutions at all levels in Nigeria, including the recently established Covenant University, where he serves as the Chancellor.

He has written over 50 titles of inspirational and motivational texts covering various aspects of life.

He is married to Faith, and their marriage is blessed with children.

## OTHER BOOKS BY DAVID O. OYEDEPO

- Anointing For Breakthrough
- Releasing the Supernatural
- Covenant Wealth
- Excellency Of Wisdom
- Understanding Vision
- Success Buttons
- Keys To Divine Health
- Born To Win
- Long Life Your Heritage
- The Wonders Of Praise
- Breaking Financial Hardship
- Exploits Of Faith
- The Release Of Power
- Walking In The Miraculous
- Satan Get Lost!
- The Winning Wisdom
- Walking In Wisdom
- Dynamics Of Holiness
- The Force Of Freedom
- The Healing Balm

- Understanding Financial Prosperity
- Emergence Of The Glorious Church
- Conquering Controlling Power
- Breaking The Curses Of Life
- Showers Of Blessings
- The Law Of Faith
- The Miracle Seed
- Keys To Answered Prayer
- Keys To Divine Protection
- Overcoming Forces Of Wickedness
- The Path Of The Eagle
- The Blood Triumph
- The Mystery Of The Anointing Oil
- The Hidden Covenants Of Blessings
- Put Your Angels To Work
- Understanding The Power Of Praise
- You Shall Not Be Barren!
- Exploring The Secrets Of Success
- Understanding Divine Direction